Lincoln Christian College

CHOSEN

COMMUNICATING WITH JEWS OF ALL FAITHS

P9-DFS-132

CHOSEN

COMMUNICATING WITH JEWS OF ALL FAITHS

LEE AMBER

VISION HOUSE PUBLISHERS
Santa Ana, California 92705

Verses marked RSV are from The Revised Standard Version of
the Bible copyrighted 1946, 1952 © 1971, 1973. Used by permission.

Information from Talmud was taken from:

Rabbinic Anthology, by C. G. Montefiore and H. Loewe, published by Schocken Books, Inc., New York, copyright 1970.

and

Everyman's Talmud, by Rev. Dr. A. Cohen, published by E. P.
Dutton & Co., New York, copyright 1949.

Chosen

Copyright ©1977 by Vision House Publishers,
Santa Ana, California 92705.

Library of Congress Catalog Card Number 77-87104
ISBN 0-88449-072-6

All rights reserved. No portion of this book may be re-
produced in any form without the written permission of the
Publishers, except for brief excerpts in reviews.

Printed in the United States of America.

To Vision House,

for having the
perspicacity,
fortitude,
audacity
and
chutspah
to publish my first book.

70948

Contents

Introduction   9

1 Torah and Talmud   15

2 What is a Jew?   27

3 Messiahs, Messiahs, Everywhere Messiahs   39

4 Where Will You Stand?   53

5 Famous Jews Only Jews Know Well   69

6 Unusual Movements in the History
   of the Jewish People   89

7 Questions and Answers 131

Introduction

I'm Jewish.

Soon after accepting the Messiah *Yeshua* (Jesus) as my Savior in 1960, the Lord laid it on my heart to begin a missionary work among Gentile Christians to help them be better able to tell my people about the Messiah. In the course of that ministry, I learned that many Gentiles who truly love the Lord have a burning desire to witness, but are hindered by lack of understanding of Jewish ways of thinking.

In church after church questions came up which clearly indicated that lack. For instance, a man once asked me if it was true that it is traditional for Jewish sons to try to steal the family business away from their fathers. Another took exception to the fact that so many Jews were becoming professional men. Others have tried to bring Jews to the Messiah on the ground that they "ought to accept Him because they crucified Him," or "because He was a Jew." Many have tried to witness to someone who's Jewish because they didn't like them and hoped that by "converting" them they could turn them into more likeable people. Of course, by "likeable" they meant more like themselves. Not very Christian reasons, any of them.

On the other hand, I found that there were Christians who had a deep and burning love for Jews because of their special position in God's scheme of things and because they truly wanted to see them saved. Some loved Jews because they knew them either through friendship or through intermarriage. Others witnessed to Jews because their Christian natures made them love everybody. Moreover, many Gentiles have been led of the Lord to tell Jewish people about their Savior out of a conviction that these are the end times, when "the full number of the Gentiles will come in and all Israel will be saved" (Romans 11:25, 26, RSV). They want a piece of that action.

It took a while for me to learn that many Gentiles harbor prejudicial ideas about my people, without actually hating them, because of what they believe to be true about them. Time after time, I have heard laymen and pastors proclaim their love for the Jews, while at the same time saying things that are most unpleasant to the ears of my people. One author, known the world over for his books on prophecy, made this statement in one of his seminars: "The Jews in the kingdom will be different than they are now. We won't have so much trouble with them."

If there were unsaved Jews in that audience, you can bet they immediately began to think of the centuries of Christian persecution of Jews and were turned off to anything he might have said after that—and it was a great Christian message. After the meeting, I spoke to him about it and he stoutly maintained his love for the Jews, insisting that I was too sensitive. He was absolutely right about my being sensitive—I'm Jewish!

You will understand more about the reasons for that sensitivity as you read on. Keep in mind that the prejudicial things that happen to us are not at all unusual. Experiences of this nature are in the background of almost every Jewish person you'll meet.

After World War II, when the revelations of what went on in Nazi Germany became known, there was a great revulsion against anti-semitism. Because open expressions of it have been rare since then, a whole generation of young Jews has grown up without really experiencing the abuse and hatred that former generations of Jews have had to endure. These young people generally do not have as much sensitivity to slights and insults as the vast majority of us do. Let's be happy for them, but let's not make the mistake of assuming that the mass of Jews has had the same experience as they have. Nor can we feel that these young Jews understand what it really means to be Jewish, simply because they were born of Jewish parents. That is a mistake many Gentile Christians are making today, with sad results. Always assume your Jewish loved ones have been victimized for their Jewishness, usually in the name of Christ, and then you will always tend to be on the loving side of them. That will put you on the Jesus side.

As you progress in this book, you will be shown what to avoid and why you must avoid it. And you will be given ways and means to show the Jewish people your love, thereby opening the door to telling them about their Messiah. You will be given Scripture from both Old and New Covenants, and practical help, too. If you will take the lessons to heart, you will have the joy of seeing your Jewish loved ones saved, "for the gospel is the power of God for salvation, to the Jew first . . ." (Romans 1:16).

As you read you will get to know Jewish people better, and your understanding and love for them will grow. You will find yourself becoming more sensitive, more conscious of the unending attacks on them. You will also find yourself more determined to defend them. Part of your ability to witness to Jews will have its roots in that willingness to defend them.

Here are a few (RSV) verses that will strengthen you in your resolve to identify with and defend Jews:

Genesis 12:3—"I will bless those who bless you and *him* who curses you I will curse." God blesses generally those who bless the Jews, but He curses *individually* those who curse them.

Isaiah 11:13b—"Those who harass Judah shall be cut off. . . ."

I Corinthians 10:32a—"Give no offense to Jews. . . ."

I Corinthians 9:20—"To the Jews I became as a Jew, in order to win Jews. . . ."

Isaiah 14:1—"The Lord will have compassion on Jacob and will again choose Israel, and will set them in their own land, and aliens will join them and will cleave to the house of Jacob."

John 13:35—"By this all men will know that you are my disciples, if you have love for one another."

As the sole object of this book is to help real Christians who desire to be among those who will "cleave to the house of Jacob" (Isaiah 14:1, RSV), you must decide whether or not you really love the Jewish people and want to help them know their Messiah. If you do, read on. If you don't, forget it. The book is so Jewish-oriented that you must really care a great deal or you'll just be wasting your time.

Now then, a word of warning for those of you who

are still with us. There are some very unpleasant facts set forth here concerning Christian activities against Jewish people. The only reason I have included them is that so many Christians are unaware of the fact that awful things have been, and are still being done to Jews in the name of "Christ." I am not trying to make you feel guilty, unless you are guilty. But, if you are guilty and are still reading, this indicates that deep down inside you care and, therefore, I can help you.

The unpleasant information is given to help you understand Jewish opposition to what you're saying and to develop in you a deep feeling of compassion and sympathy for Jews. Without this, you will not have enough love, and love is the key to opening the hearts of any people—Jewish or otherwise.

I John 4:20, 21 (RSV)—"If anyone says, 'I love God,' and hates his brother, he is a liar; for he who does not love his brother whom he has seen, cannot love God whom he has not seen. And this commandment we have from Him, that he who loves God should love his brother also."

> "Take upon yourselves the yoke of the kingdom of heaven, vie one with the other in the fear of God and practice loving deeds toward one another" (The Talmud: Sifré Deut. 323; 138b).

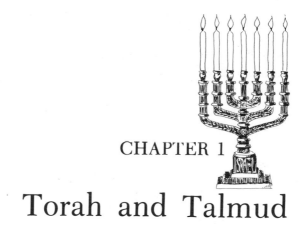

CHAPTER 1

Torah and Talmud

Torah

The history of Torah is the history of the Old Testament, because the Torah, for most Jews, consists of the five books of Moses (or, as it is sometimes called, the Pentateuch). Some Jewish groups add other books, usually from the prophets, but for the majority of knowledgeable Jews the Torah consists of Genesis, Exodus, Leviticus, Numbers and Deuteronomy.

Talmud

The Talmud is a collection of the opinions of the sages of the ages. Second to the Torah, it has been the guiding light for my people. Back around 200 B.C.E. (Before the Common Era—B.C. in our terms) Jewish scholars decided to collect and write down all existing commentaries on the Old Testament. They gathered together the oral law and tradition, handed down mostly by memory through generations of Jews, and added discussions about these same issues by the most prominent Jewish wise men of their own time. This collecting activity went on for some 400 years, and the result was a hodgepodge of information which was badly in need of systematic organization.

Judah Was A Prince

The job of organization. was undertaken around 200 c.e. (Common Era—a.d. in our terms) by one brilliant scholar, Rabbi Judah Hanasi ("the Prince"), whose work codifying all that ancient material is now called the Mishnah ("Instruction"). In the centuries that followed, other scholars added their comments to the Mishnah, and the result is the Talmud. It is primarily a commentary on the Mishnah that, like little Eva, "just growed."

Present-day scholars generally believe talmudic thought began to take shape rather haphazardly back in the days of Nehemiah and Ezra, after the Babylonian captivity. These two leaders found a book of the Law in the ruins of Jerusalem (Nehemiah 7:5). They discovered, to their amazement, that people wanted to know about the Law and how to apply it to their everyday problems. The people didn't care so much what it meant, only how to make it fit their needs. This created a demand for teachers to interpret the Law and teach it to the people. As time went on, the number of teachers grew and soon they themselves became objects of commentary by other rabbis.

Everyone Wants to Get into the Act

All of this adding of commentary on commentary on commentary was done mostly by memory. There was even a professional class of memorizers called Tannaim, whose job it was to keep all the talmudic information in their heads and teach it to the upcoming generation. One reason memorizing was so important was simply that writing materials were scarce and very expensive. Finding enough materials to record such a vast amount of information was beyond the ability and means of the scholars of the day.

Organizing and codifying the various levels of commentary was a monumental task. We have to give Rabbi Judah Hanasi credit for even undertaking it, let alone completing it. But complete it he did, and thought that was that. It wasn't. Soon afterwards more scholars were commenting on the Mishnah and on one another. Their commentaries, called Gemara ("studies") were combined with the Mishnah to produce the Talmud.

Old Slewfoot into the Act

However, beginning around 200 B.C., efforts to wipe out the Jewish people became increasingly strong. Every time a Jewish scholar was eliminated a great mass of memorized material was lost with him. So it became desirable to have all one's thoughts in writing. A little here and a little there, the commentaries of rabbis grew in mass over a period of four centuries, roughly from 200 B.C. to A.D. 200. It was this accumulation of written information which Judah organized into the Mishnah.

Now let's review this process. First, there is the work containing all the oral, written, general and traditional information from the beginning of Jewish history, gathered together initially by memory, later in writing, and finally codified by Rabbi Judah Hanasi. This is the

Mishnah. Second, there is the series of commentaries on the Mishnah, collected and written down by later scholars for another three hundred years, called the Gemara. Finally, the whole of it is called the Talmud.

The Lord into the Act

While all this was going on, Jewish history was proceeding as well. After the fall of Jerusalem in A.D. 70, some scholars in Palestine were separated from those who went to Babylonia. Each group continued to put together the ancient teaching. As communication was poor in those times it was impossible for all of them to work on only one rendition. As a result, two Talmuds came into being. Since the majority of learned rabbis located in Babylonia, the *Babylonian Talmud* was much more complete than the *Jerusalem Talmud* and became known as THE Talmud.

The People into the Act

Talmud has two main parts. One part contains references to the Law, and is known as Halakah. The other part contains references to everything but the Law, that is: customs, traditions, anecdotes, explanations, theories, stories, history and all other facets of Jewish life down through the ages. This is called Aggadah or Haggadah.

Organizing and writing the Talmud was not always fully approved by the Jewish community. The Sadducees around Rabbi Judah's time were opposed to it on the ground that no man was smart enough to reinterpret Scripture just to suit the needs of the people at any given time. The Pharisees, being more sympathetic to these needs, were for it. The Sadducees lost out. Yet, work on Talmud was stopped for a time on the ground that all that was necessary had already been done. But the desire of these ancient sages to express themselves was so strong that the commenting eventually began again. In addition, the people continued to demand interpretations to settle their problems. This enabled the teachers to develop themselves into an elite class, which was very profitable for them.

Rabbis into the Act

So you see, the growth of the Talmud didn't proceed smoothly and without interruption for hundreds of years. Such a thing just wasn't possible. For instance, around A.D. 35 the rabbis of the day became concerned that certain new oral laws would eventually replace Torah in popularity, so they insisted those laws be memorized instead of written. It wasn't until later that these were written and included in the Halakah portion of the Talmud.

Scholars varied in their view of how the Law should be approached. In the first century B.C.E., two great rabbis, Shammai and Hillel, got into an argument about the proper attitude toward the laws. Hillel was president of the Sanhedrin, Shammai, vice-president—the two most important Jewish scholars of their time. Shammai was sternly legalistic, while Hillel leaned toward more lenient interpretations with emphasis on human rights. As you might have expected, Hillel walked off with the blue ribbon. People then, as now, prefer to shape the law to suit their own desires. This debate, while Hillel and Shammai lived and for centuries afterwards, inhibited the writing down of oral law.

History into the Act

Then history added a new impetus for writing down Talmudic thought. The Roman Empire began to come apart—barbarian hordes took over in the Middle East. Jews and Christians alike were murdered in vast numbers. Once again Jewish scholars died and with them was lost a large slice of memorized, collective Jewish knowlege. This forced the rabbis to reconsider their position, and as before, those memorized laws and other information began to go down on parchment.

The Curtain Closes on the Act

But finally, around A.D. 700, the work was considered to be complete. Re-editing, reinterpreting, re-codifying went on until around the year A.D. 1600, but no new information was added.

The Talmud today consists of three main parts: the Mishnah, the Gemara and the Midrash. The first two have already been described. The Midrash is the loveliest portion of Talmud because it expresses the sages' love of God and Torah through passages on the Bible, wise sayings and sermons.

If one could memorize the entire Talmud, he would be very knowledgeable on every facet of life, from medicine to poetry. It's because Jews in earlier days were taught Talmud from the age of two until they were grown that we survive as a people today. The men who worked on the Talmud through hundreds of years claimed they were inspired by God. This is true at least in part, for it is through the learning handed down in the Talmud that God protected the Jewish people. At crucial times in our history we survived only because our enemies desperately needed our knowledge. talmudic lore is so extensive and complex we cannot begin to describe it in any more detail. There have been scholars who have spent their entire lives becoming experts in just one tractate (book) of the 63 in the *Babylonian Talmud*. Nevertheless, you now have a pretty good idea of what the Talmud is and how it came to be. May God bless it to your Christian life.

Comparisons Between Talmud and New Testament

We've discussed the Talmud and its origins. We have also stated the belief among my people that it was divinely inspired (although it is not generally believed to be infallible). Now the time has come to teach you how closely the Talmud parallels New Testament teaching. The knowledge you are about to receive will be of inestimable value in your efforts to reach your Jewish loved ones for their Messiah. It will help bridge the gap that has sprung up between Jews and Christians over the years because of incorrect teaching and other misunderstandings.

In His Sermon on the Mount, Jesus tells us: "Not an iota, not a dot of the law shall pass from the law until all is accomplished" (Matthew 5:18, RSV). It is not generally appreciated how closely Messiah's teaching actually followed the Law as it is interpreted in the Talmud. Following are just a few examples. The teaching from the Talmud will be listed first, followed immediately by its counterpart from Holy Scripture. Only New Testament quotes will be used, as the point is to show that *Yeshua* (Jesus) agreed with His ancestors. Each quotation will have listed with it its scriptural or talmudic reference. Those from Talmud will reflect the consensus of opinion, not just that of one or two rabbis. Always remember that where the Talmud is quoted, *it's the consensus of opinion that counts*, because many conflicting opinions may be recorded. Also, references should be insisted upon for purposes of clarification, because quotations taken out of context can be quite misleading. Space restricts us to the use of only a relative few of the many hundreds of talmudic statements which are completely supported by our Lord's words.

On God

"God requires more than intellectual acceptance; He demands moral obligation" (Berachoth II 2). "Faith, by itself, if it has no works, is dead" (James 2:17, RSV).

God has no bodily form and "sees the work of His Hands but they cannot see Him" (Midrash 217a). "God is spirit, and those who worship him must worship in spirit and truth" (John 4:24, RSV).

"In every place where you find the imprint of men's feet there am I (Mechilta 52b). "Lo, I am with you always, to the close of the age" (Matthew 28:20, RSV).

"God knows all minds" (Berachoth 13c). "I am He who searches mind and heart" (Revelation 2:23, RSV).

"God knows what is to be in the future" (Sanhedrin

90b). "No prophecy ever came by the impulse of man, but men moved by the Holy Spirit spoke from God" (II Peter 1:21, RSV).

"The world is judged by grace" (Aboth III.19). "The righteous shall live by faith" (Makkoth 24a). "For by grace you have been saved through faith" (Ephesians 2:8, RSV).

"My Holiness is higher than any degree of holiness you can reach" (Rabbinical Leviticus XXXIV. 9.). "All have sinned and fall short of the glory of God" (Romans 3:23, RSV).

"The Holy One . . . created the universe accordingly . . ." (Rabbinical Genesis 1.1). "All things were made through Him. . . ." (John 1:3, RSV).

"There are righteous men among all nations who will have a share in the world to come" (Tosifta Sanhedrin XIII.2). "Whoever lives and believes in me shall never die" (John 11:26, RSV).

On Satan

"You should say, 'May the all-merciful rebuke Satan,' " (Kiddushin 81 a, b). "The archangel Michael, contending with the devil . . . said, 'The Lord rebuke you' " (Jude 9, RSV).

"Satan performs the function of seducing men, accusing them and killing them" (Baba Bathra 16a). The New Testament on "seducing": "False Christs . . . will arise . . . to lead astray . . . the elect" (Mark 13:22, RSV). On "accusing": ". . . for the accuser of our brethren has been thrown down, who accuses them day and night before our God" (Revelation 12:10, RSV). On "killing": ". . . nor grumble, as some of them did and were destroyed by the Destroyer" (I Corinthians 10:10, RSV).

On Marriage

"Marriages are made in heaven" (Sotah 2a). It is God who joins a man and a woman in marriage (Mark 10:9).

"Among those who cry but nobody notices is the husband who is ruled by his wife" (Baba Metzia 75b). "Likewise ye wives, be submissive to your husbands . . ." (I Peter 3:1, RSV).

"A man may not divorce his wife except for unfaithfulness" (Ketuboth III 5). "Whoever divorces his wife, except for unchastity, and marries another, commits adultery" (Matthew 19:9, RSV).

"If one refrains from punishing a child, he will end by becoming utterly depraved" (Rabbinical Exodus 1.1). Also, "A man should not terrorize his children" (Gittin 6b). "Fathers, do not provoke your children to anger, but bring them up in the discipline and instruction of the Lord" (Ephesians 6:4, RSV).

The Talmud goes on at length about honoring father and mother (Peah 1.1, Kiddishin 30b, 31b). Ephesians 6:2 and other passages repeat the commandment: "Honor your father and mother."

On Man

"It is senseless to seek nothing but wealth" (Eccles. R. v 14). "What does it profit a man, to gain the whole world and forfeit his soul" (Mark 8:36).

"Store up treasures in heaven by means of worthy actions" (Aboth 6:9). "Lay up for yourselves treasures in heaven, where neither moth nor rust consumes and where thieves do not break in and steal" (Matthew 6:20, RSV).

"God gave us a soul: if we don't keep it pure, He'll take it from us" (Niddah 30b). "Do not fear those who kill the body but cannot kill the soul; rather fear him who can destroy both soul and body in hell" (Matthew 10:28, RSV).

"There is no death without sin" (Shabbat 55b). "The wages of sin is death" (Romans 6:23, RSV).

"Repent one day before your death" (which means now, because you don't know when you'll die) (Shabbat 153a). "Behold now is the day of salvation" (II Corinthians 6:2, RSV).

On the Soul

"The soul is the spiritual force within man which inspires him with ideals and prompts him to choose good over evil" (Taanith 27b). "May your . . . soul be kept sound and blameless at the coming of our Lord (I Thessalonians 5:23, RSV).

"Blessed art Thou, O Lord, who restores souls to dead bodies" (Ber. 60b). "Lazarus, come out . . ." (John 11:43, RSV).

On the Coming Messiah and the End of the Age

"Wait for Him. When you see . . . many troubles coming upon Israel" (which implies the reestablishment of the state of Israel) (Sanhedrin 97a). "Judges and officers of the law will have no authority; denunciators will multiply; anarchy will reign supreme" (Shabbat 188a).

"Among the wise men there will be constant strife" (Ketuboth 112b).

"The law [of God] will no longer be studied; those who fear sin will be despised; the house of public convention will become a house of harlots" (crooked politicians) (Sotah 49a and Sanhedrin 97a).

"There will be no respect or concern for the elderly." "The teachers' learning will become decayed and perverted" "Poverty and famine will be on the increase." "Money will be out of control." (All of the last four are in Sanhedrin 97.)

There are many other Talmudic comments on the coming Messiah and the end of the age, but these should give you an idea of just how close to the truth these sages were. Obviously, they were getting help from a higher source, and we are able to receive untold blessings from their guidance and knowledge. May these readings from the Talmud give new breadth to your Christian experience.

CHAPTER 2

What is a Jew?

Well, what *is* a Jew anyway?

I began this erudite tome (big, smart book) with the words "I'm Jewish," trusting that my readers would mostly be sweet, kindly, loving Christians who wouldn't say, "Prove it." So far, no one has, praise the Lord! I could prove it all right, but it would take a lot of time and effort, so I'm glad no one has asked. Yet, in a book about things Jewish, how can one proceed without establishing that Jewishness really exists.

Abe Was Gentile Until . . .

Down through the ages countless attempts have been made to define Jewishness, and now I'm about to make another. But I feel my definition has some backing from the Creator of Jewishness. We'll talk more about that later. Meantime, let's go back in history to the person most people consider to be the first Jew, Abram (Abraham). He believed the Lord and it was "counted unto him for righteousness" (Genesis 15:6).

Abram did this in an age when practically everyone else was an idolater. Evidently a taste for his kind of righteousness has something to do with Jewishness, because before he "believed God" Abe was a Gentile.

Are there other kinds of proof of Jewishness? It's generally conceded that we Jews today are physically descended from Abraham, Isaac, and Jacob. The latter was renamed Israel by the Lord and his name is used throughout Scripture to indicated those who are heirs of Jewishness, either by birth or through the Messiah, whose function was, and is, to take care of "righteousness" for us when we ask forgiveness and tell Him we accept Him as Messiah.

But, if one is a Jew only if he is descended from these three, with no other considerations, what do we make of Sarah, Rebecca, Rachel and Leah. All of these wives of the "Patriarchs" are considered to have been Jewish, though they obviously were not descendants of the three original *gahntze machers* (V.I.P.'s), Abraham, Isaac and Jacob.

In the Beginning

When we read the story in Genesis we find all of them in a close personal relationship with God and trying to do His will. The point seems to be there were others besides Abraham who believed God, and it was counted to them, too, as "righteousness." They were all involved in this business we call "Jewishness." Further proof? Well, Jacob had a twin brother called Esau who didn't believe God. It is recorded that God rejected him out of the Jewish heritage even before he was born (Genesis 25:23 and Romans 9:7-13). God knew how it would be with him and cast him out, even though he was the firstborn and his father, Isaac, preferred him to Jacob. Esau's children became the Edomites, and their descendants are among the worst enemies of Jews.

But is "righteousness" all there is to being Jewish? A study of Jewish writings indicates that God considers a background of respect for His Law, reverence toward Him, repentance of sin and belief in His Son—Messiah (Isaiah 7:14 and 9:6; also the Talmud, Sukkah 52a) to be prerequisites for Jewishness. So to the patriarchs it was not just a sense of personal fellowship with God, but also a certain style of religious thought that marked a person as Jewish.

Yet, there also seems to be something unique going for us who are physical descendants of the three Patriarchs. God has a special place in His heart for us, because we were the first people chosen to carry the message of the true God (Romans 11) and, despite some defections from Him, we managed to get that message across. Witness the early church—they were all Jews.

What's Jewish Already?

So well now, let's examine things more closely for other clues as to what physical Jewishness is.

The Talmud says anyone born of a Jewish mother is Jewish (Kiddushin 68a,b), regardless of any other considerations, such as, adopting another religion, failing to live in Israel, or so many other ideas that cause one Jew to say to another, "You're not Jewish." But the vast majority of my people today are not convinced by the Talmud—or perhaps they are not familiar with what it has to say on the subject. In fact, in a survey of 1500

Israeli families, conducted by the Jerusalem *Post* back in 1968, and published on November 25th of that year, these were the answers to the question, "What is a Jew?":

12%   Anyone whose father or mother was Jewish or has a Jewish mate
23%   Anyone who says he's Jewish
19%   Anyone who has a Jewish mother, or is a convert
13%   Anyone who lives in or identifies with Israel
13%   Anyone who follows some form of Jewish religious practice
11%   Anyone raised or educated as a Jew
 9%   No opinion (in other words, they couldn't even come up with an answer)

David Ben Gurion, called the architect of modern Israel and its first prime minister, answered the same question: "A Jew is a Jew is a Jew is a Jew. . . ." He meant there is an eternal something about being Jewish that defies description. But is that something Jewish really indefinable? We must remember that neither Ben Gurion nor the majority of those polled by the Jerusalem *Post* were believers in *Yeshua* (Jesus) as Messiah. Therefore, it hadn't occurred to them to ask the Creator of Jewish people for His ideas on the subject. I thought to ask.

The Answer

Following is an answer to the question "What is a Jew?" which is the result of much prayer on the subject. I understand it is not a complete definition, because our finite minds simply cannot grasp the total implications of what the Lord did when He created what we humans have called "Jewishness." It's similar to the concept of being "born-again." We know being "born again" is a genuine experience, but how or why it works we can't answer. Is it a chemical or electrical process? Who can say? Some day we'll know all there is to know about it, but, for now, it's beyond our abilities to comprehend. And a definition of Jewishness is similar and for the same reasons.

However, I would like to share with you what the Lord gave me. I'm confident that it's valid and that it can help you better understand what makes us Jews tick. This, in turn, is bound to improve communication between you and your Jewish loved ones, and that will surely help them see Messiah more easily.

In this definition I am referring to those who declare themselves to be Jewish by reason of birth or Jewish religion, and not those who consider themselves to be Jewish by reason of faith in Yeshua, the Jewish Messiah. After all, it's your *unsaved* Jewish loved ones you have such a burden for and, therefore, you want to know as much about *them* as possible. And so, here is my answer to the question "What is a Jew?"

1. Ancestry

A Jew must be a descendant of Abraham, Isaac and Jacob. The Talmud acknowledges that sincere proselytes are true Jews (Sifra to xviii. 5). However, this applied only before Messiah (Christ), in a time when Jewishness was rooted in God-given Law; Torah reigned supreme. In those days Gentile converts to Judaism became true spiritual Israelites and God recognized them as such (Exodus 12:48,49). "It was counted unto them for righteousness," even as it is today, when Gentiles accept the Messiah.

Converts to modern Jewish religions aren't in that same position, because those religions themselves have turned away from what the early Patriarchs of Judaism said were God's intentions. They believed that if people repented of their sins there would be a Son-Messiah who would bring them into a personal relationship with God (Exodus R.XV.21, Joma 86a and others in Talmud; Isaiah 9:6 in Scripture). The "righteousness" inherent in true "Jewishness" as set forth in Scripture and Talmud is no longer imputed to Gentile converts to modern Judaism, but only to those who trust Messiah to be their righteousness. Probably that's one reason why it's difficult for us real Jews to communicate with these Gentile converts to Judaism as we would with another Jew. The *yiddishe saichel* (Jewish mindedness) just isn't there.

From Goyim to Gerim [1]

I have, however, known Gentiles who acquired this Jewish mindedness through:
   A. the acceptance of *Yeshua* as Savior
   B. asking forgiveness for sin
   C. hard work and determination to learn all about things "Jewish."
Evidently, *yiddishe saichel* can be a part of the "righteousness" imputed to believers, if they care enough about it to go after it prayerfully.

---

[1] Hebrew, meaning a Gentile convert to Judaism.

But what about those who have Jewish ancestry but have not accepted what God did for us in our Messiah? Do they have this "righteousness"? About all that can be said is that we're born with an aptitude for it, like a light that's plugged in, but turned off. "Well," you may say, "if that's so, why is it that more of them haven't accepted it down through the ages?" A study of our history reveals that thousands of us *have* accepted it. Speaking in terms of percentages of total ethnic groups, there's a strong possibility that a larger percentage of Jews have been saved through the centuries than of any other group. And it is an interesting fact that this has been recorded mostly by Jewish rather than Christian historians. Evidently, that's the reason most Christians are unaware that it has been happening.

From Darkness to Light

And it has happened even in some of the worst periods in our history, when we suffered abuse in the name of Christ. On the surface, it may appear that it is the figure of Jesus Himself that turns my people off, but when one digs deeper he finds that it's really the result of fear, anger and resentment at the treatment we have endured in His name. This is surely proven by two facts:
1. Thousands of us have been saved in spite of harsh treatment in Jesus' name.
2. In modern times, with anti-semitism at a low ebb, especially in the United States, Jews are accepting Jesus as Messiah faster than ever before in our history.

The evidence seems to show that if you love us, you're

two-thirds of the way toward overcoming our fear and
bringing us to God's righteousness."

2. Religion

A Jew may practice some form of modern Jewish
religion, but it isn't strictly necessary (Kiddushin 68
a,b). Many of my people will dispute this, but it's a fact
that Jewishness does not depend on religious practice.
We all know Jewish people who never go near a synagogue, yet they are Jewish, no doubt about it.
However, I strongly advise that you avoid arguments
over this matter, because you may win the argument
and lose the soul.

3. Race

Jews are a race in a spiritual sense only. There was a
time when Jewishness could be described in physical
terms, but since the Dispersion this is not possible. We
now have black Jews, white Jews, Indian Jews, Chinese
Jews and—well, you name it. I have met and talked
with Indian and Chinese Jews and they are true Jews.
As I said earlier, what it is that makes them so is a
mystery.

4. Temperament

The emotional make-up of Jewish people is different.
This is illustrated by the Jewish languages (Hebrew and
Yiddish), which are far more expressive of feelings than

most other languages. It is also borne out by the Old Testament. The ancient Hebrews were constantly torn emotionally between their desire for Jehovah and their desire to excite the flesh like their neighbors were doing. Those neighbors had no such problems. They simply chased idols as much as they pleased with hardly a thought for God. Furthermore, a study of our history and of the Talmud shows conclusively that the capacity of my people for love far transcends that of other unsaved people. Other peoples have benefited tremendously from this, as is seen by comparing our contributions to the world with the world's contributions to us.

5. Mentality

The Jewish mentality is distinctive. There is a wider diversity of thought among us, stemming, no doubt, from that intense emotional system I just mentioned.

Another interesting indication of the unique Jewish mentality is the fact that one seldom meets a really unintelligent Jew. One may meet Jews who are unlettered, untrained and uninterested in the things of the mind, but seldom will he encounter an unintelligent Jew. It's well known that the quality and quantity of our intellectual achievements in relation to our numbers in the population is out of all proportion. Unfortunately, this makes the average, unsaved Gentile jealous, rather than grateful. But, one of the things I noticed when I accepted my Messiah was that Gentile Christians, in contrast to unbelieving Gentiles, were grateful to my people for their contributions to society. To me, that indicated that something was different about them. Now I know it to be an expression of that certain

something which began with Abraham and which we
call "righteousness."

The Jewish mentality is also reflected in our inherent gentleness of disposition. Police records show the
incidence of violent crime among Jews to be very low,
compared to our numbers in the population. The Bible
records that the ancient Egyptians were able to overcome and enslave the Israelites even though the
Israelites were "too many and too mighty" for them (Exodus 1:9). It's true that in the battles for Israel today my
people fight with great effectiveness, but after Hitler
and the "Holocaust" of six million who died for no
other reason than that they were Jews, we feel we have
our backs to the wall. Even so, it is recorded that, in
most cases, the Arabs were amazed at the gentle
treatment they received at the hands of their Israeli
conquerors (see chapter 6).

6. Instinct

This is the most difficult of all to pinpoint. There is
a kind of tribal instinct among us that makes us need
each other. Put one of us in a crowded room and we'll
feel more at home if we know other Jews are present.
Even among us Jewish Christians the instinct is at work.
We have to be with other Jewish people from time to
time, or a sort of homesick feeling comes over us that
will not be denied. I have seen Jews, both saved and unsaved, try to deny this feeling, or even ignore it, but
eventually it has an effect on their lives. Look at Moses.
Forty years raised in the Egyptian court as a prince of
Egypt, and eventually he gave it all up and went back
to being what he was—a Jew.

So there you have it, the answer to the question "What is a Jew?" You'll notice I've said nothing about appearance, habits, accents, ideas or any of the other external characteristics that the world sees as "Jewish." That's because these things are the result of environment and upbringing, rather than being part of the inherent makeup which God has constituted in true Jewishness. As such, they are easily altered by circumstances, often to a radical extent. That's why the nation of Israel is having such difficulty molding the people who come there through *aliyah* (the ingathering of world Jewry to Israel) into one cohesive culture. Their backgrounds and experiences in life are too many and varied for this desirable goal to be easily accomplished. Basically, however, they do have the inherent attributes we discussed, and that's what keeps Israel trying and slowly succeeding. That, and the determination of Almighty God not to let us perish.

You may not agree with all this at first, but I think if you'll pray about it the truth will be confirmed in your heart.

> "Whoever prays on behalf of a fellow man, while himself being in the need of the same thing, will be answered first" (The Talmud, Baba Kamma 92a).

CHAPTER 3

Messiahs, Messiahs, Everywhere Messiahs

From the time of the "Teacher of Righteousness" (described in chapter 4) until the 19th century, many of my people have been eagerly waiting for Messiah. At various propitious moments in history Satan has given them "messiahs" who, of course, have disappointed them.

Menahem bar Judah—6-70 C.E. (A.D.)

One of these was Menahem bar Judah. This fellow actually captured the fortress of Masada, which established pretty good credentials for messiahship among the sages of the age. So he went to Jerusalem to take on the Romans. Lo and behold, he licked the Roman garrison there, too. This brought the main Roman armies into the act. It also made the other power seekers in Jerusalem jealous, so they killed him. Poor Menahem.

Simeon bar Kozibah (Kokhba)—second century C.E.(A.D.)

Probably the greatest of all the aspirants to the office of Messiah. For 60 years following the fall of Jerusalem and the destruction of the Temple (70 C.E., or A.D.) the Romans behaved with such inhumanity that a major new revolt finally broke out. There had been smaller ones right along, but this was a main event. It was triggered primarily by the determination of Emperor Hadrian to remove the Jews and all vestiges of Judaism for all time from the face of the earth.

When it became apparent what was afoot, an inspired military leader named Simeon bar Kokhba gathered an army together and rebelled. For three years, from 132 to 135 C.E., the Jewish armies made mincemeat of the Romans and very nearly freed Judea from Roman rule. The Jewish effort was so strong that Hadrian finally realized that if the revolt was not put down the rest of the world might get the idea the Romans weren't invincible after all and that would be the end of the empire. So he called in his greatest general, Julius Severus, mustered the mightiest army the Romans ever fielded and, after a battle lasting several months, finally defeated and destroyed the last Jewish garrison at a fort called Betar. Bar Kokhba died in the fighting, but at the height of his success he had been named as the promised Messiah by no less a personage than Rabbi Akiba ben Joseph, one of the greatest Jewish scholars of all time. There were other scholars of the time who disagreed with Akiba, and it looks as though they were right after all.

One important development came out of bar Kokhba's revolt. Up to this time Jewish Christians had worshipped freely in the temple. But when they refused to accept his messiahship they were politely (and not so politely) asked to leave. This is how the church of *Yeshua* the Messiah became separated from the worship of Rabbinical Judaism. Poor Simeon. Poor Akiba. Poor everyone.

This sort of thing went on until today the expectation of a coming Messiah is almost completely dead among the Jewish people generally; exactly what the prince of this world wanted to happen. Of course, in the last several years many thousands of us have recognized that *Yeshua* is Messiah, but there are millions left who do not. So, I'm nudging (nagging) you to go tell them.

With the death of bar Kokhba the hope for Messiah was smothered for quite a few centuries, until around 800 c.e. Then it started again.

Christianity had taken over the masses, the Dark Ages were beginning, and we Jews, with our educated ways, were in demand. The age of mysticism was well under way, so it seemed a good time for another "messiah" to come. So, one did.

Abu Isa—eighth century

Abu was an illiterate tailor who, nevertheless, was credited with writing books on God, Law, Torah and Talmud. Abu gained a few admirers, but since he really was illiterate, he didn't last long. To be a successful "messiah" in those days you had to read and write, in order to curry favor with the ruling class (who couldn't read or write). Poor Abu.

After Abu, the "messiah" business fell on hard times. Maybe the idea got around that you had to prove it. Anyway, nothing happened until the 12th century, when up popped another.

Ibn Aryeh—12th century

He was apparently a Christian who dreamed one night that he was It. Ibn got along fine with Jews, even while preaching the gospel (honest!), but then he decided to go to North Africa to preach to the Moslems. They beat him to death. Poor Ibn.

Moses Al-Dar'i—1127 C.E.

In that year, Moses declared himself a prophet and advised the people to sell all they had, because Messiah was coming at Passover time. After Passover, Moses escaped to Israel, where he died. His movement actually began in Baghdad, Persia (now Iran). Poor Moses.

David Alroy—12th century

He declared himself "messiah" and induced the Jews of Persia to rebel. At the head of a large force, he attacked a fort near his hometown and lost. It is suspected he was killed by his own father-in-law. Even in those days fathers-in-law expected sons-in-law to be successful. Poor David.

The Yemenese Messiah—12th century

This fellow invented some new prayers. They must have been impressive, because quite a few Jews and even Arabs flocked to the fold. Then he made a mistake. He told some doubting Arabs that if they cut off his head he would immediately come back to life. They evidently were curious about it—so they did. Poor Yemenese "messiah."

(On the Kabalistic Messiahs, see chapter 6 on Kabala. Some were rather impressive for a while.)

Abraham Abulafia—1240-1291

Abe's ancestry from a noble Spanish Jewish family interfered with his messiahship. He heard a voice which declared him to be a prophet, but no one believed him, so he took off for Jerusalem. On the way he heard another voice which told him Pope Nicholas III was in reality Jewish, so he turned around and headed for Rome. There he actually got an audience. The news of his supposed conversion to Judaism so excited and angered the Pope he had a heart attack and died. Abe was headed for the stake, but he quickly did some mystic Kabalistic talking and was released. Quite a trick for a Jew in those days, even if he was a "messiah." The rabbis still wouldn't take him seriously, so he went off in a huff. He not only went off in it, it swallowed him up. Poor Abraham.

Abraham ben Samuel—around 1300

This Abe saw himself as "messiah," but also as a messenger of the Messiah. He wavered back and forth so much he got everybody confused. If he had stuck with one claim or the other, his act would have had a longer run, so eager were the people for Messiah to come. However, his inability to decide caused people to laugh at him and that was the end of his story. Nowhere does Scripture or Talmud say the Messiah will be a comedian. Poor Abe.

Martin Luther—16th century

In all fairness, it should be pointed out that Luther was never considered to be the Messiah, but only His forerunner. At the beginning of his reformation Luther was very partial to my people, thinking they would be more inclined to accept *Yeshua* as Messiah if treated kindly. As a result some Jews saw him as Messiah's messenger. But when the majority rejected his advances, Luther turned violently against the Jews and quickly lost his job as forerunner. Actually, his original plan was working, but communications were poor and he didn't know it was working. The record shows that many Jews came to the Lord Jesus in the early days of Lutheranism. Historians tell us that Martin became sick, feeling depressed and unheeded in his later years. Being bitter, he turned on the Jews. I submit that Martin, being uninformed, got frustrated about us and turned on us. It was then that his ministry began to deteriorate. I further submit that much of the great work he did for the Lord is counter-balanced by his latter-day hatred for the Jews. Poor Martin.

Asher Lemmlin—16th century

He awoke one morning and discovered he was a prophet. The people, however, decided he was the

Messiah. Even his grandfather was persuaded and disposed of everything he couldn't use in the messianic kingdom. The people adored Asher for a while, but when he failed to conquer the world after a few months they deserted him. Presumably, including grandpa. Poor Asher.

David Reuveni—16th century

Reuveni was a dwarf with a great flair for show business. He rode into Venice on a beautiful white horse and claimed he was the brother of the king of the lost tribe of Reuben. Pope Clement VII believed him. He also claimed to have an army of thousands of Jews who were following the Turkish Army into Europe. And he offered to place this army at the disposal of the Pope, so that he could drive out the infidel Turks. The Pope checked with the king of Portugal, an authority on the Far East, and the king certified that Reuveni was the real thing. European Jews were delighted and quite certain the Messiah had come at last. Thousands of Marranos (Spanish Christian Jews) returned to their Jewish origins and many thousands of Gentiles converted to Judaism. Meanwhile, the Inquisition began to take note of these people and the king and Pope themselves became upset at what was happening. Reuveni, being the smart little fellow he was, took off for Italy, while the Marranos and converts to Judaism went up in flames.

In Italy, Reuveni again tried to set himself up as the king of the tribe of Reuben, but this time he was dealing with Emperor Charles V, who believed wholeheartedly in the Inquisition. Charlie put Reuveni in irons, and after that he disappeared from history. He probably was allowed to die slowly in prison, which probably was some improvement over going to the stake. Poor David.

Solomon Molko—16th century

Sol originally wasn't even Jewish, but the idea of being the Messiah was so appealing in those days he decided to get into the act. Although he knew nothing of Judaism, he converted, boned up on the Talmud a little and set himself up as a prophet. The Inquisition wasn't healthy for prophets, so he skipped out to Palestine, where in a few years he acquired a smattering of Kabalism. When it seemed safe, he returned to Italy, where he declared himself the Messiah. He was such a convincing fellow and such a great preacher that the Inquisition was forbidden to touch him.

Then Sol made a mistake. He joined with David Reuveni and had to deal with Charles V. Since he wasn't Jewish by birth, Charley gave him a chance to recant. But Sol had convinced even himself he was the Messiah, so he refused and promptly went up in flames. Poor Sol.

Sabbatai Zevi—1626-1676

Zevi had the good sense to show up at the end of the Thirty Years War, when all Europe reeked with the stench of blood and the people had had their fill of butchery.

Sabbatai was no itinerant beggar of a would-be

"messiah." He had the finest of educations and was fluent in at least three languages: Hebrew, Arabic and Turkish, his native tongue. As a youth he had become interested in Kabala, and soon he was so holy he began to hear voices. Isn't it interesting how many would-be "messiahs" hear voices? Sabbatai's voices must have been convincing because he declared himself the Messiah and immediately began to abolish all the old laws and customs that the rabbis had painstakingly built up over the centuries. The people adored him. Those laws had become unbearable, because there were almost as many of them as there were followers of Sabbatai Zevi (over a million). Well, perhaps I exaggerate about the number of laws, but you know what Jesus said about the unbearable burdens the rabbis were putting on the people. Jesus was only talking about the laws that existed then. More were added as the centuries rolled by.

So Sabbatai prospered. There was a tradition that the Messiah would marry a harlot, and on a trip to Egypt that's what Zevi did. According to historians of the day, she was very beautiful, but I suspect they just put that in to embellish the story.

Zevi continued to evangelize the Middle East until, finally, the rabbis proclaimed him a fake. Nobody believed them, except the Sultan of Turkey. When Sabbatai arrived there, the Sultan clapped him in irons and gave him the choice of death or becoming a Mohammedan and being set free. Sabbatai did the practical thing. He converted. But later he found that he just couldn't give up being the "messiah," so the Sultan threw him back into prison and there he died. Even after his conversion to Mohammedanism, his followers clung to him and until the day he died they came to his prison cell to worship him. I won't say,

"Poor Sabbatai." He was a pretty successful "messiah," as messiahs go. In fact he left his mark on Jewish history. Since his time, all those myriad laws have been more or less ignored by most of my people.

Jacob Frank—18th century

After Sabbatai Zevi, a real bona fide villain took over the mantle of "messiah." Jacob Frank was a traveling salesman and, judging from his activities, he may have been the one who started all those jokes about traveling salesmen. According to Jake, anyone could be saved by being pure, and the way to get purified was by going to bed with Jake. He certainly made it pay. The people showered him with money, which he used to live in the grand style. The rabbis finally excommunicated him because of his activities, which included seances combined with sex orgies.

After that, he was given an opportunity to leave Turkey, where he had engaged in most of his activities. He wisely accepted and went to Poland, where the Jewish community would have nothing to do with him. They were about to put him out of business, but his followers appealed to the local bishop. He sided with the Frankists because of their determination to destroy the Talmud. They actually did destroy one copy of the Talmud, which was quite a feat in a day when copies of anything were hard to come by, mechanical printing presses being few and far between.

As a result of the bishop's action and the schism within the Jewish community in Poland, many thousands of Frankist Jews entered the church and were absorbed into Gentile society through intermarriage or just plain loss of their Jewishness.

As for Jake, he was thrown into prison for preaching that the Holy Trinity consisted of Father, Holy Spirit and Sabbatai Zevi, and he stayed there for 13 years. When Russia invaded Poland, he was set free and went to Austria—where he started all over again. The Austrians thought he was wonderful and he lived there until the age of 66, when he died of apoplexy. All the other false "messiahs" had something going for them that might have given the people reason to believe in them, but not Jacob Frank. He was pure charlatan through and through, and showed it. Perhaps, it was his personality or the promise of salvation through sexual freedom that made him popular. Whatever it was, it worked for him—at least in this world. If we could see where he is now and what he's doing, I'm sure we would come away with a different picture. Poor Jake.

Baal Shem Tov ("Master of the Good Name") —18th century

His real name was Israel ben Eliezer, and he was born about 1700 in the Ukraine.

According to one school of thought there are many events in this man's life that are reminiscent of Jesus. This school claims that when his parents were quite old, an angel appeared to them and told them they would have a son who would carry God's messages to man on earth.

They died when Izzy was very young, and the boy was cared for and given an education by the community, as was required by Jewish law. His early manhood, according to reports of his followers, was spent in poverty and in the working of such miracles as healing the sick, walking on water, and exorcising ghosts out of people. They claimed he could release souls from Hell, although how they knew when this had been accomplished is not explained.

Of course, there are other reports that claim he was a stupid lout who wouldn't work and amounted to nothing until proclaiming himself the Messiah at the age of 42.

I'm inclined to believe the latter because of the form of Judaism Shem Tov founded—Hasidism.

The Talmud says that from the age of six on a child should be stuffed with Torah like an ox (Baba Bathra 21a), but Hasidism encouraged ignorance as the best kind of piety. This kind of thinking dealt a severe blow to rigid adherence to Torah and Talmud. Shem Tov taught that the way to God was not through thought, learning, and hard work, but through personal ecstatic experiences. Can you imagine how the people ate that up? Its followers believed Hasidism turned utter defeat into total victory. Weaklings were supposed to become towers of strength. It sounds similar to Christianity, except that Hasidists tried to do it on their own power and therefore failed. We Christians, of course, do it in God's power, so we succeed.

The impossibility of a person saving himself through his own strength became apparent when Shem Tov died. The movement was unable to find a man with sufficient charisma to take his place. Within two centuries it was destroyed by its own internal dissensions. At one time, this form of Judaism had well over a million adherents. *It is not to be confused with present day Hasidism, which adheres strictly to the law of Torah and Talmud.*

Moses of Crete—5th century

This genius of the "messiah" industry promised to walk the Jews of Crete across the Mediterranean to the promised land without anyone even getting his feet wet. And hundreds of them believed him. He really never had much of a future as a "messiah," however. He just couldn't keep from getting people in over their heads. Poor Moe.

Nap, the Verbrennter (an extremist)

In addition to the foregoing, there have been many others whom small groups of rabbis declared to be the Messiah from time to time. None of these is of much importance historically, except Napoleon Bonaparte. Upon becoming emperor, Nap made things easy for the Jews, who had been having it rough for many years. Accordingly, the rabbis took a look at his record in conquering the world and decided he was It. By that time, the "messiah" syndrome had run its course, so nobody believed the rabbis except the rabbis. As for Nap, he ended up a bust. Poor Nap.

CHAPTER 4

Where Will You Stand?

We've emphasized Jewish sensitivity and the reasons for it because if Christians want to know what makes us Jews tick that is one element they must understand and accept. Showing Christian love for my people is a must if you want to tell them about their Messiah in an effective manner. Love overcomes the unpleasant memories that Satan often uses to keep people from seeing the Savior as He really is. And love accomplishes something else, too. It helps us learn not to express and think many of the things that might be turning someone off to the beauty of God.

> "Love is patient and kind; it is not arrogant or rude. Love does not insist on its own way; it is not irritable or resentful; it does not rejoice in wrong, it rejoices in the right" (I Cor. 13:4-6, *RSV*).

In short, everyone gets saved faster with love.

In this chapter we'll discuss some commonly used expressions and ideas the Jewish community considers to be anti-semitic. They are so prevalent there's no need to feel personally guilty about them. But one must be honest and face up to whether or not they are rooted in

real, geniune, honest-to-goodness, down-to-earth everyday anti-semitism. If so, and one can honestly admit
it—great! Once admitted, give it to the Lord who
"cleanses us from all sin" (I John 1:9). After all, we are
required to "give no offense to the Jews" (I Cor. 10:32),
or to anyone else, for that matter. So now, let's keep a
firm grip on our love for one another as we try to rid
ourselves of ideas my people consider to be detrimental
to their well-being. We'll begin with the word . . .

Jew

That tiny little word can arouse some very negative
emotions in the minds of many Jewish people when they
hear it bandied about in the Gentile world. I remember
from early in my life the foul expressions directed at me
that began with the word "Jew," usually including the
word "Christ" and frequently including my mother.
And this wasn't unusual; it happened to the majority of
Jewish people of my generation as they grew up. Grant-
ed, it isn't always possible to avoid saying "Jew"; it
would make you stilted and uneasy in your Messianic
explanations to my people. But do try to avoid using it
wherever possible. I've seldom used it in this book,
because I want you to be able to give the book to your
Jewish loved ones so they'll know that real Christians
are willing to make great efforts to understand and
spare their feelings.

But how does one avoid using the word "Jew"? A
person isn't a Jew; he's Jewish. My people aren't Jews;
they're Jewish. "Jews" as a group aren't this or that, although some Jewish people might be. Get the idea?
Now, practice a few expressions such as, "I love the

Jewish people. And if I don't love any Jewish person, I'm going to ask Jesus to help me learn to love all people who are Jewish because He does." There now, that wasn't so hard, was it?

The Jews

The emphasis here is on the two words used together, like this—"THEJEWS." Have you ever noticed that when John Smith is dishonest people say, "John Smith is a crook," but when somebody Jewish is dishonest they say, "Those Jews are all crooks"? Haman (in the Book of Esther) was a prime example of that sort of thinking. One Jewish man, Mordecai, refused to bow to him and he promptly set about murdering all the Jewish people in the kingdom. No descriptive words apply to *all* Jews. So, you mustn't be at all surprised when talking to a Jewish friend if he disagrees with something I've said here. "Well then," you ask, "what do I do?" The ideas set forth here are *guidelines only*, but they will apply to the vast majority of Jewish people. However, remember that your final authority is God, who works very efficiently when love is flowing, because He *is* love (I John 4:8).

Talmud and New Testament agree that if we don't love our fellow man we can't love God because, "in the image of God made He man" (Genesis R. XXIV.7., Talmud, and I John 4:20). They also agree that human beings are individuals and to overlook that is to disrespect God, because He made each one unique (I Cor. 12, and Genesis R. XXII.6., Talmud).

Satan uses our willingness to group people by leading us to notice the sins of a few and then blame them on the group as a whole. When we do that we begin to dislike the whole group, and that interferes with our ability to present the Messiah with love. And when we don't present Him with love, folks aren't likely to accept Him. When that happens Satan rejoices, but that doesn't mean he's going to be grateful to us and treat us more kindly. So we might as well treat people as individuals in the first place. That way we'll at least outsmart the old boy . . . for a short time, anyway . . . we hope.

Christ or Messiah?

If you mix with Jewish Christians you'll find us using "Messiah" among ourselves. The idea is to make it easier for our unsaved brethren to accept what we have to say about Him. In fact, for reasons already mentioned, most of us try to stay away from the words "Jesus" and "Christ" as much as possible. When talking to most Jewish people it's best to use *Yeshua*. If they ask what that means simply explain it's the Hebrew word for "Jesus," both meaning "salvation." Sometimes, if you know the person well enough to feel he won't object, He can be called the "Messiah Jesus," but usually it's best simply to say *Yeshua*. And, if you really want to impress, learn to say *Yeshua ha Meshiach* (YehSHOOah hah MehSHEEahch) meaning, "Jesus, the Messiah."

Try to avoid the word "Christ." Jewish people are aware that Gentile Christians have been using the word "Christ" all their lives. However, unfortunately, non-Christians have also been using it—as a swear word against our people. For them, "JEWCHRISTKILLER" is all one word and many of us can remember hearing it three or four times a day, every day. The habit of using the name "Christ" will not be easy to overcome, but if one practices at home or among family and friends, God will honor the effort and help. I know this from Gentile Christians who have tried it and told me of their success. After a while one begins to prefer "Messiah." It has a softer, more pleasing feel to it.

It bears repeating that not all Jewish people are so deeply affected by these words. But enough are that we suggest again that you play it safe. Using the word "Messiah" is not a denial of Christ. We are merely following Paul's teaching, "to the Jews I became as a Jew that I might win Jews (I Cor. 9:20, RSV).

Family Jokes are for the Family

Jewish people may often tell "Jewish" jokes in the presence of non-Jews, yet, they'll be uneasy when those same non-Jews do likewise. Most people realize family jokes can only be told by family and aren't funny when told by outsiders. Even we Jewish Christians must be careful, for many unbelieving Jewish people consider us to be outsiders for having accepted a "Gentile religion." Frankly, many Jewish Christians don't enjoy hearing non-Jews tell Jewish jokes either. We're Jews and have Jewish sensitivities. Besides, we're concerned that if it's done in our presence it will be done in the presence of Jewish unbelievers. When ethnic jokes are told in Christian gatherings, *which happens all too often*, there is a VERY good possibility there *will* be Jewish unbelievers who will hear it. Anyone making any sort of bigoted remarks in church or elsewhere should be gently and lovingly rebuked, especially teachers and pastors.

Jews are Cheap

According to a survey made by *Fortune* magazine and published in its issue of January, 1966, the Jewish people give more to organized charities per capita than any other ethnic group. And that isn't just to Jewish charities, that's to all charities. The Talmud says, "Our Rabbis have taught, 'We must support the poor of the Gentiles with the poor of Israel, visit the sick of the Gentiles with the sick of Israel, and give honourable burial to the dead of the Gentiles as to the dead of Israel, because of the ways of peace' " (Gittin 61a). So, through many centuries charitable donations have become traditional with us. While not all of us are aware of the talmudic origins for our behavior, most know that giving generously is "Jewish." The Hebrew word for alms-giving is *tzedakah*, "righteousness." The rabbis insisted that even those who receive charity must also give to charity (Gittin 7b).

We Jews are the only ethnic group that has organized charities in nearly every incorporated area in the United States, and those charities usually take care of all in need, regardless of race, creed or color. Publishing such statistics has never seemed to alleviate the prejudice Gentiles have about Jews and money, but Christians should realize that if a person believes Jewish people are cheap, Satan will bring enough cheap Jews into his life to keep him convinced. Those Christians who have dealings with *many* Jewish people know that, by and large, we are a generous, warm-hearted people.

May I suggest that those of you who have a problem with this (and this includes many Jews who themselves have such a prejudice) go directly to God for the truth.

We have seen a number of Christians cured of false conceptions about ethnic groups by doing just that. "If any of you lacks wisdom, let him ask God who gives to all men generously and without reproaching, and it will be given him. But let him ask in faith, with no doubting" (James 1:5, 6a, RSV). "Come now, let us reason together, says the Lord" (Isaiah 1:18, RSV).

Jews All Have Big Noses

On a recent trip to Israel I checked this one out. Now, as a supereminent authority on noses, I can state without equivocation that Jewish noses are pretty much like noses anywhere. Some people, even in Israel, do have large noses, but I didn't meet anyone who wanted to be reminded of it. On the other hand, lots of folks have such small noses one wonders how they breathe. Incidentally, non-Jews with big noses can be sensitive about it, too. My father-in-law was hurt all his life by jibes about his nose—and he was a Gentile!

Jews Talk With Their Hands

A young Gentile Christian girl once said to me that I wasn't like other Jews because I didn't talk with my hands. Others who were present pointed out that the French and Italians tend to do that. I simply asked her if it wasn't possible that she was automatically assuming that the people she saw using their hands were Jewish because she believed that Jews talk with their hands. That stumped her.

But this incident brings out an important factor in

the whole business of how we think about people. The saying "Seeing is believing" isn't entirely true. We don't believe what we see, we see what we believe. So it is with ethnic groups. People think we Jews have big noses, talk with our hands, have accents or whatever, and so, the only Jews they recognize are the ones with these characteristics. But the vast majority of Jewish Americans don't fit into this picture, although there is a fairly small minority that do.

But what of it? Christ loves us all, complete with the characteristics He built into us. And wouldn't the world be dull if we were all exactly alike?

According to the Talmud, man's individuality declares the greatness of God: "A man strikes many coins from one die and they are all alike. But God strikes every person from the die of the first man, but not one resembles another" (Sanhedrin 38a).

Jews are Sharpies in Business

There is a vow many religious Jewish people say at Yom Kippur when asking forgiveness for their sins of the previous year. It contains the words: "All our vows shall not be vows, all our promises shall not be promises." Throughout the centuries this has been used by our enemies as evidence we do not consider a promise made to a Gentile as binding. This vow, called "Kol Nidre" ("All Vows," or "Our Vows"), was devised as a prayer many centuries ago and it is strictly between the individual Jewish person and the Lord. It has nothing whatever to do with human relationships. What it really does is ask God to overlook the vows made to Him during the year which the individual has not kept.

According to the Talmud every Jewish person is required to be completely scrupulous in his dealings and this applies especially to dealings with Gentiles. Not to do so is to profane the name of the Lord—in other words, to commit blasphemy, the unforgivable sin (Tosifta B.K. X.15). Police records reveal the percentage of Jewish people convicted of felonies involving dishonesty in business dealings is lower by far than their percentage of the population. I can just hear the diehards saying, "See? That shows how sharp they are. They don't get caught." What can you do?

"The Protocols of the Learned Elders of Zion"

This purports to be secret evidence of a plot among Jewish leaders to take over the world. In spite of its having been proven a fake time and time again, some of our country's most prominent men have tended to believe it. Back in the early 1920's the Ku Klux Klan, with an assist from Henry Ford's newspaper, the Dearborn *Independent*, tried to give credibility to it. But this effort failed when Ford, realizing he was in error, apologized to the Jewish community.

"The Protocols," published in 1903, came into being because Czar Nicholas II thought that by making scapegoats of the Jews he could take the minds of his subjects off their miseries. He commissioned a monk named Sergei Nilus to invent something sufficiently damning that it would turn the gathering fury of the peasantry away from himself. The Russian peasants weren't fooled for long, but the "Protocols" have since become a favorite tool of professional Jew-haters.

There have been many investigations of these

documents, and they have invariably proven them to be a fraud. One of the most thorough was by the United States Congress. The results, which completely repudiated the "Protocols," are now a part of the Congressional Record (inserted August 6, 1964). In spite of this repudiation, anti-Jewish forces repeatedly attempt to show the "Protocols" to be valid *because* they're included in the Congressional Record. Among these anti-Jewish forces are some who peddled their hatred in the name of the Messiah; for instance, Gerald L. K. Smith's Christian Nationalist Crusade. Is it any wonder that many unsaved Jewish people are turned off to listening to Christians? How are they to know the difference unless *we* show them patience, kindness, understanding and love?

The Diaspora [1]

What are the facts about so-called "world Jewry"? There are about 14 million Jewish people in the world. One-fourth of these are in Russia, where they are virtually prisoners and fear daily for their safety. One-fourth are in Israel, where they are surrounded by hostile neighbors and must be constantly on the alert for attacks from those neighbors. This keeps them fully occupied.

That leaves about five million right here in the Unites States, plus scattered remnants in other parts of the world. So, here we are, born and raised in different cultures, speaking many different languages, with widely divergent ideas, hopes, dreams and aspirations, totaling less than one-half of one percent of the pop-

---

[1] World Jewry outside of Israel.

ulation of the world. And we're supposed to take it over? If we were up to it, we surely would have done so when Hitler was busy wiping out some forty percent of our people. The truth is, we were so disorganized that if the Christian world hadn't come to our rescue we would have been completely annihilated. For a fact, we're so fragmented that even Israel is having great difficulty melding the Jewish refugees who come there into a unified whole, in spite of the fact most of them are fugitives from persecution.

We've talked about the danger of thinking in terms of "the Jews." The "Protocols" argument is just another form of it. And lately, Israel's enemies, with their oil money, have been disseminating this document all over the world, in hundreds of languages.

To close, I'd like to teach you an old Jewish proverb, so that when you hear about such things as "The Protocols of the Elders of Zion" you'll remember it and have yourself a laugh:

> *"A zis do svei hidden, zis do drei krigenzagt."*
> (Wherever there are two Jews there are three arguments.)

The Jews Killed Christ

This is a whole subject unto itself, but for now, a few verses should help get the matter into perspective. Scripture makes it clear that the Jewish people themselves loved the Savior (Matthew 21:9 and 26:4, 5). This made the chief priests envious, so they, along with some renegade Pharisees, decided to do away with Him (John 11:48, 49). Gathering together some of the soldiers of the temple, and enlisting a Roman cohort of soldiers (300 to 600 men), they sent them to seize Jesus. When Peter attempted to defend Him he was told, "Do you think I cannot appeal to my Father, and He will at once send me more than twelve legions of angels?" (Matthew 26:53, RSV). In an earlier discourse the Lord had said, "For this reason the Father loves me, because I lay down my life, that I may take it again. *No one takes it from me, but I lay it down of my own accord.* I have power to lay it down, and I have power to take it again; this charge I have received from my Father" (John 10:17, 18, RSV).

Thank God that in our day most believers recognize that the Savior died for us all because we are all equally guilty of sin (Ecclesiastes 7:20; Romans 3:23). Because real, born-again Christians believe this and are showing great love for my people Israel, we are accepting *Yeshua* as Lord in greater numbers than ever before.

For those who insist that the Jewish people alone are guilty of the blood of the Messiah, let me ask you this question: Is He dead? If you think so, say this little prayer, "Lord, forgive my sins; I accept Jesus (or *Yeshua*) as my Savior." Do that, and you will find out how alive He really is—and you will be saved in the bargain.

Jews Control the "(You Name It)" Industry

We *are* achievers out of proportion to our percentage of the population. I believe this is a gift from God, lest our burden be too much to bear. But can it be said that we *control* everything? Investigate any industry, science or profession where Jews are prominent and you'll find we are vastly "out-prominented" by Gentiles through sheer force of numbers. This is yet another form of the "the Jews" syndrome. The cure to this distorted thinking? Well, let's remember a pebble on the beach gets a lot of our attention if we step on it, but if we don't step on it we don't notice it.

Jews are Loud and Pushy

What this really means is that some people resent it when we defend our rights both legally and as human beings. Far from forcing their way into places where they're not wanted, most Jews learn from early childhood not to do that because we realize we wouldn't be happy there anyway. It's interesting to note that while we are accused of being pushy we are at the same time accused of being clannish. By and large we don't want to do that either, but if forced into a choice, "clannish" will probably come out on top.

The fact there is discussion among Christian Jews about forming their own churches proves we'd rather just go off by ourselves than get involved in battles with our opposition, even though clannishness is really un-Jewish. ("Separate not yourself from the community," says the Talmud [Aboth II.5]). To date, the Jewish church movement isn't very strong, but I can see it really exploding if the prejudices I've discussed in this chapter aren't overcome. And wouldn't that be unfortunate? What church hasn't been blessed by the Jewish Christians in its congregation?

To some extent all ethnic groups tend to be clannish. People simply are more at ease with those who share their own culture and traditions. Yet, as those old ties fade into memory with the passing generations we

Jews have always become a part of the culture in which we lived—when we were allowed to, that is. (Note: according to the Jewish newspaper, *Israel Today*, there are only three-fourths as many Jews in the United States today as there were a generation ago. Intermarriage and the dropping away from traditional ties are among the main reasons.)

Jews Really Know the Old Testament

The ones who do are few and far between. Look at it this way, how many Gentiles know the New Testament? Unsaved people are unsaved people, and there is no reason to expect an interest in the things of God from them just because they're Jewish. Of course, there are scholars who study the whole Bible from an intellectual point of view, but that doesn't mean they're saved or are going to be, especially if no one tells them about the Messiah.

In Israel we had a tour guide who was very well versed in the New Testament, almost an expert. He needed the information in his work, so he acquired it, but he had no faith in it. All his technical knowledge wasn't saving him. He had no intimate personal relationship with God the Father, because he had never asked His Messiah to come into his life and forgive his sins. His knowledge was helpful to me, however, in my efforts to tell him about the Lord. You may meet someone like this, but you mustn't assume that all Jews are so well informed.

Jews Sacrifice Gentile Babies at Their Religious Services and Drink Their Blood

Can you imagine anyone in his right mind believing

this? Well, they do. FACT: In Russia, in 1913, a Jewish laborer named Mendel Beilis was tried for the ritual murder of a young Gentile, in spite of the fact it was proved the crime had been committed by a gang of juvenile thieves. He was finally acquitted, but he was tried on the charge *after* the real killers had been found. And the lie lives on.

FACT: In 1928, officials in Massena, N.Y., questioned the town rabbi about ritual slaying, because of the disappearance of a child. To be fair, it must be pointed out that national indignation was aroused against the police officers involved.

Immediately after World War II, this idea fell into disrepute, but now it's being propagated again with the use of Middle East oil money. We Jewish Christians are of the opinion that as the return of Messiah draws closer we'll be hearing more of this sort of thing. What makes this accusation especially absurd is the fact that the Torah expressly forbids the consuming of blood (Leviticus 17:10 and Deuteronomy 12:16). Furthermore, talmudic dietary laws go into great detail concerning the complete removal of blood from meat. Meat with any blood in it is absolutely not kosher, and the consumption of blood is a great sin (M. Keritot, the beginning).[2]

I remember in my teens being invited to the home of some Gentile (non-Christian) friends for dinner and being served soup made from the blood of a goose. To be polite, I tried to eat it, but I became quite nauseated and very nearly retched. Evidently the revulsion against eating blood continues to be very Jewish. And why not? The Word says the children of God shall not consume blood. *Yeshua* is the Word (John 1:1), and He is "the

---

[2] George F. Moore, *Judaism in the First Centuries of the Christian Era* (Cambridge, MA: Harvard University Press, 1927), Vol. II, p. 74.

same yesterday and today and forever" (Hebrews 13:8). So, if you're a Christian and want to know just how Jewish your Christianity is, try eating blood—but be sure and have a basin handy when you do.

Jews Talk with a Brooklyn Accent

If they were born and raised in Brooklyn they do. They also talk with New York accents, southern accents, midwestern accents, Canadian accents, northwestern accents, Mexican accents, Russian, French, German, Indian, Chinese, Turkish, Philippine, English, and wherever else they've been dispersed to, accents. In Israel, they even speak Hebrew with these accents. There, now! I've admitted it and I'm glad.

Messiah Is the Answer

In concluding this chapter, let me say that the fact that these accusations are made can be of great help to you in your relationships with Jewish loved ones, because they make Christian love and concern much more meaningful. All my experience with abuse in the name of Christ was wiped out when I encountered real Christian love. Read I John 4:16, and you'll realize just how powerful Christian love can be. It's God at work in you and is very impressive indeed. I know. It got me into the Kingdom and made me happy to be a Jew for the first time in my life!

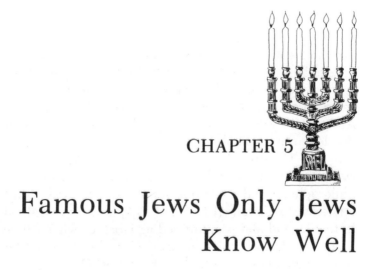

CHAPTER 5

Famous Jews Only Jews Know Well

The Lord has impressed me that a believer who wants to be sensitive to my people needs to know about some very famous Jews that aren't part of public knowledge. Everyone has heard about Albert Einstein, Henry Kissinger and Jonas Salk. (What? You mean you didn't know he discovered the polio vaccine? Oh! You didn't know he was Jewish.) But there are others who are most important in Jewish history. Your knowing about them will please your Jewish loved ones. Even if they have never heard of them, they'll be pleased that you know about them. If they have heard of them, they'll still be pleased that you took the time to find out about them. Study these people; you can only gain by it.

Moses ben Maimon (1135-1204)

More popularly known as "Maimonides" (myMAHNideez); also known as "Rambam." Born in Cordova, Spain, Maimonides was one of the greatest, if not the greatest, of Jewish geniuses. He was an expert in law, philosophy, medicine, astronomy, and logic. At the same time he was the acknowledged head of world Jewry in his day. He was fluent in Spanish, Hebrew and Arabic. His code on Jewish law, called *Mishneh Torah* is divided into 14 books and is an authoritative work to this day. He wrote, in Arabic, a book called, *Guide to the Perplexed*, which is still widely influencing philosophers and religious thinkers. He was court physician to Caliph Al Fadal of Egypt. He is enshrined in folk legend and is entombed in Tiberias, where there is an inscription which reads, "Here lies our master Moses ben Maimon, Mankind's Chosen One."

Alfred Dreyfus (1859-1935)

A Jewish officer on the French General Staff, his name became generally known to the public, but the details of his history are not known to many Gentiles. In 1894, Dreyfus was tried for treason when papers were discovered which he was supposed to have written. The case became one of the most famous in legal history and brought on a major struggle between the forces of anti-semitism and those of decency and fair play. Dreyfus was convicted. But as time went on further evidence was uncovered that the papers were really written by a Major Ferdinand Esterhazy, also on the army's General Staff. The French army, to cover up its mistake, prevailed upon the government to suppress the evidence. As a result, Dreyfus was disgraced and imprisoned on Devil's Island.

The fight was continued, however, and finally a famous author, Emile Zola, became convinced that Dreyfus was innocent. His publication of a paper entitled *"J'Accuse"* ("I Accuse") forced a reopening of the case and a second trial. By this time, Dreyfus' innocence was common knowledge and it was thought he would be exonerated. However, the court again found him guilty and sentenced him to ten years in prison. The entire world became outraged at this obvious miscarriage of justice. Under public pressure the President of France pardoned him shortly thereafter. That didn't settle the matter, however, and the battle for his complete exoneration continued.

Finally, in 1906, the evidence of his innocence was so overwhelming that the French Supreme Court of Appeals declared him guiltless on all charges. He was reinstated in the French army as a major.

The monumental injustice involved in the Dreyfus case completely destroyed the forces of organized anti-semitism in France and also resulted in the separation of church and state in that country. The case also paved the way for a Jewish statesman to become premier of France. Leon Blum, who fought for Dreyfus during the years when hatred of Jews was at its zenith in France and who doubtless endangered his own life and career for doing so, later was elected premier of France three times. The beauty of this story is that Dreyfus lived to see that his suffering had not been in vain.

Theodore Herzl (HERtsl) (1860-1904)

Born in Budapest, Hungary, Herzl was the founder and prime mover for Zionism, or *aliyah*—that is, the in-gathering of my people to Israel. At the time of the Dreyfus case he was a reporter for the *Neue Freie Presse*, a leading newspaper of the day. The sheer injustice of the case and the obvious anti-semitism involved shocked him into the conclusion that the only answer for the Jews was a Jewish national homeland in Palestine. Herzl wrote a book called *Judenstaat* ("Jewish State") and began to seek financial help. He approached Jewish financiers of the day, among them the Rothschilds, but received no help. In 1895, he received encouragement from a Paris physician named Max Nordau, who also was famed as a writer. In 1896, his book was published and was an immediate sensation. The idea of a Jewish national homeland in Palestine caught on, and he became the leader of a movement in that direction.

On August 27, 1897, the first Zionist Congress met in Basle, Switzerland, and was attended by 197 delegates from all over the world. From this meeting came the World Zionist Organization with Herzl as its president. There were five Zionist congresses after that and out of them came the Jewish Colonial Trust, the banking arm, and the Jewish National Fund, which purchased land in Israel. Herzl carried on extensive diplomatic negotiations and received the moral support of Germany's Kaiser Wilhelm II, the Sultan of Turkey, the King of Bulgaria, King Victor Emmanuel III of Italy and several British statesmen. Pope Pius X turned him down. He worked so intensely that he finally ruined his health and on July 3, 1904, he died. Fifty years later the State of Israel was officially formed (May 14, 1948). The remains of the "Father of Israel" were flown to the Jewish state about a year later and on August 17, 1949, he was laid to rest on Mt. Herzl in Jerusalem.

Hillel *(first century B.C.E.)*

Hillel is revered as one of the greatest teachers and talmudic scholars of all time. He lived in the first century before the Messiah, was a leader of the Pharisees of that time, and was appointed head of the Sanhedrin by King Herod. He was truly a saintly man whose concern for the common people brought him the respect and love of the nation. As he would have been judged under God's Law at that time (as written in the Torah) it is more than likely that he is saved and will be with us in Paradise.

He led the Jewish people for forty years and taught them to love peace, each other, and the Torah. Most of my people will have heard of Hillel, but few of them will have any further knowledge about him. All, however, have a healthy respect for his name, and when you show that you have something more than a passing acquaintance with him, that respect will be extended to you.

Samuel Gompers (1850-1924)

Gompers was born in London and immigrated to the United States at the age of thirteen. He was a menial laborer and worked as a cigar-maker. But he soon rose to greater influence. He was a pioneer in the labor movement and organized the Cigar Makers International Union, which actually became the model for many other trade unions. He was a prime mover in the founding of the American Federation of Labor and, except for one year, was its president until he died.

Gompers refused to become involved in political disputes, insisting that the only legitimate concern of trade unions was for better wages, working hours and working conditions. Gompers has something in common with Hillel in that his is a name almost every modern Jewish person has heard but can't quite place.

Sholom Aleichem (1859-1916)

His real name was Sholom Rabinowitz. He was born in eastern Europe in what is now Soviet Russia. He was a genius who so excelled in his studies that at the age of 17 he was earning a living as a teacher. Sholom knew the Jewish Bible by heart and, although not a rabbi, was able to perform many rabbinical functions. He devoted his life entirely to writing after he suffered severe losses in a business venture, and he wrote hundreds of stories, novels and plays. Much of his work has been condensed into one volume, *The World of Sholom Aleichem*. His most famous story has become one of the most successful musicals in theatrical history—"Fiddler on the Roof." This play has educated millions in the habits, customs and sufferings of Eastern European Jewry, a subject on which Scholom Aleichem was an expert.

Simeon bar Kokhba (early second century)

A study of the career of bar Kokhba gives insight into what the people expected of the Messiah. He was a great general who in three years (132-135 C.E.) nearly succeeded in freeing Palestine from the Romans. The revolt was provoked by efforts of the Emperor Hadrian to assimilate the Jews into the Roman culture and religion (paganism) in order to end their continued efforts at rebellion. When the armies of bar Kokhba drove the Romans out of Palestine and freed Jerusalem, even Rabbi Akiba, one of the greatest of the talmudic scholars of the time, proclaimed him to be the Messiah.

Hadrian, in order to end the revolt, appointed his most able general, Julius Severus, and equipped him with the very finest Roman legions and equipment. Severus adopted a strategy of surrounding individual towns and villages and starving them out. In this way he gradually reduced bar Kokhba's holdings until he was finally cornered at a village called Bethar. There bar Kokhba held out against the seige for about a year, but he was finally defeated by hunger, thirst, and internal squabbling and treachery.

The Talmud relates that at the fall of Bethar so many people died that the blood flowed like a stream for over a mile to the sea. Over a half-million died there and many more were sold into slavery.

An interesting sidelight to bar Kokhba's leadership is that there is a letter, found in the Dead Sea caves near Qumran, in which a woman of the day wrote to bar Kokhba, complaining that her husband had married her for her money and asking the "Messiah" for justice.

Flavius Josephus (37 C.E.-105 C.E.)

Born Joseph ben Mattathias into a royal and priestly family and very well educated in the schools of the Pharisees and Sadducees, Josephus became the leading historian of his times. While he was a young man, he lived at the court of Nero, where he became impressed with the power and destiny of Rome. Upon returning to Jerusalem he found the country ready to rebel against the Romans. Josephus did everything he could to prevent the rebellion, but was unsuccessful because Roman oppression had become so odious. He then pretended to sympathize with the rebellion and, as a result, was made commander of the Jewish army in the district of Galilee. In his own account of those days,

Josephus contradicts himself, saying in one instance that he was sent to Galilee to persuade the people to lay down their arms and in another that he went there to fortify Galilee for battle. In any case, Galilee was finally captured by Vespasian near the end of the year 67. When Josephus was brought before him, the Jewish general saved his neck by pronouncing that Vespasian would one day be emperor of Rome. Much to the good fortune of Josephus, the prediction came true and when Vespasian took the throne Josephus was given Roman citizenship and was treated very generously. This was continued by his son, the Emperor Titus, after Vespasian died in A.D. 79.

Vespasian appointed Josephus to be official historian for the Roman Empire and his works survive to this day. They are: *History of the Jewish Wars* (about the wars against Rome), *Antiquities of the Jews* (a history of the Jewish people), *Against Apion* (answering a famous Jew-hater of the day) and *Vita* (a reply to another historian who accused Josephus of being a traitor to his people because of his loyalty to Rome).

Viscount Edmund H. Allenby (1861-1936)

Not many people know that this world famous Field Marshal was Jewish. When World War I broke out, Allenby commanded the British cavalry in France. Later, he commanded troops in North Africa. He captured Jerusalem, defeating the Turks and setting Palestine on the path to becoming the State of Israel. He was helped by troops from an English fighting unit called, the "Jewish Legion."

Rebecca Gratz (1781-1869)

Even my people don't generally know about her, but I give the information to you as a sort of bonus. This will help you show that you really do know something about Jews that even most Jews don't know.

Rebecca Gratz was an internationally famous beauty who was also noted for her intelligence and sweet disposition. She did a great deal of writing and was active in her community and in Jewish work. Her beauty was so great that she was painted by many famous artists.

Emma Lazarus (1849-1887)

She was a native American, born in New York of a fairly wealthy and influential family. The treatment of Jews in Europe and especially in Russia inspired her literary talents and she became a famous poetess. Part of her work, "The New Colossus," is inscribed on the Statue of Liberty:

> Not like the brazen giant of Greek fame,
> With conquering limbs astride from land to
>   land;
> Here at our sea-washed, sunset gates shall stand
> A mighty woman with a torch, whose flame
> Is the imprisoned lightning, and her name
> Mother of exiles, From her beacon-hand
> Glows world-wide welcome; her mild eyes
>   command
> The air-bridged harbor that twin cities frame.
> "Keep ancient lands, your storied pomp!" cries
>   she

With silent lips, "Give me your tired, your
poor,
Your huddled masses yearning to breathe free,
The wretched refuse of your teeming shore.
Send these, the homeless, tempest-tossed to
me;
I lift my lamp beside the golden door!"

Yehudah Hanasi (about A.D. 130-220)

Hanasi is more generally known as Judah the Prince.
After Hillel, he was the greatest of all talmudic
scholars. So gentle and God-like was this man that he
was known as the "Holy Rabbi." During four centuries
preceding his life, Jewish oral law had grown and
become a part of Jewish life. Judah the Prince compiled
all this law into a set of writings which we Jews now call
the Mishnah (see chapter 1). He edited and classified
the rabbinic writings, and the work he did has come
down to us virtually unchanged to this day. He was a
modest and humble man, who gave generously to the
poor and who loved learning and teaching. He was
quoted as having said, "I learned most from my
students." He is known to have loved them deeply.
Judah was the last of the Tannaim, that great body of
scholars who compiled the Talmud.

The Others

There are many other influential Jews whom I
would like to mention briefly. Some of these names you
will no doubt recognize, but some of them may be
pleasant surprises for you.

Luis de Torrez: Reputed to be the first of Columbus' crew to set foot in the New World.

Judah P. Benjamin: Secretary of State for the Confederacy.

Sidney Hillman: Prominent in the American labor movement. First chairman of the Political Action Committee of the C.I.O.

Julius Rosenwald: Father of the mail-order business in the United States. He gave generously to many civic causes; among them, the establishing of a fund of $30 million to promote Negro welfare.

David Sarnoff: One time president of the Radio Corporation of America.

Nathan Straus: One of the founders of R.H. Macy & Company. Through his efforts our children drink pasteurized milk. Also known for his philanthropies.

Bela Schick: Devised the Schick test for determining if diptheria is present.

Samuel Leibowitz: Successfully defended and obtained the release from prison of the "Scottsboro boys." These four Negro youths had been falsely accused of rape. They were poor and unable to defend themselves and Mr. Leibowitz went to the rescue.

Joseph Pulitzer: Editor of the St. Louis *Post Dispatch* and the New York *World*, two of the country's great newspapers. Established the Pulitzer prizes for excellence in literature and the arts.

Adolph Ochs: Built the New York *Times* into the great newspaper it is.

Irving Berlin: The dean of modern American composers. It's impossible to list the hundreds of song hits he has to his credit. Three of the most famous are, "God Bless America," "Alexander's Ragtime Band" and "White Christmas."

Sholom Asch: Author of *The Nazarene* and *The Apostle.* There are many who believe that Asch was a true believer in Messiah *Yeshua.*

Rabbi Stephen S. Wise: World famous religious leader and onetime president of The American Jewish Congress. He was famous for his battles for human rights.

Karl Marx: Born to Jewish Christian parents; raised in the Lutheran church; founded Communism.

George Woolf: One of the world's leading jockeys.

Lawrence E. Steinhardt: Prominent as an ambassador to many countries, among them Sweden and Russia.

FAMOUS JEWISH CHRISTIANS

In the first century, most of the believers that Jesus was Messiah were Jews. This included the Apostles, the Disciples, and many thousands who were "completed" at Pentecost. Down through the centuries a remnant has been saved and become part of the New Covenant (see Jeremiah 31:31-33).

Nineteenth century historians have estimated that over 200,000 Jews became Christians at that time. In our generation so many Jews have come to the Lord it has not been possible to keep track of them. Our people are alarmed by it, but that's because they persist in thinking that Jews who "convert" cease being Jews. We Jewish Christians are working overtime to convince them "it ain't so."

Following are the names of some persons who, though Christians, were still very Jewish in their feelings, sympathies, and backgrounds. In short, if it walks Jewish, talks Jewish, thinks Jewish, acts Jewish and loves everything Jewish, it's Jewish. We Jewish Christians maintain that anyone descended from Abraham, Isaac and Jacob is Jewish. So does the Talmud, if the descent is through the mother. We believe it because it's scriptural and that's our answer to the accusation that Jewish believers are no longer Jewish. It should be your answer, too.

Benjamin Disraeli (1804-1881)

One of the great men of British history, Disraeli was twice prime minister, leader of the Tory Party and chancellor of the exchequer. Modern Jewish scholars claim that Disraeli became a Christian at the age of twelve to avoid persecution as a Jew, since anti-semitism was prevalent in England at the time. However, a study of his writings reveals that he was a believer who never lost his love for his people. He had great sympathy for the working classes and was instrumental in obtaining passage of many progressive laws pertaining to the well-being of the common people.

On a larger scale, he proclaimed Queen Victoria Empress of India, obtained a controlling interest in the Suez Canal for England, and arranged for Cypress to be ceded to the Empire. He was a favorite of the Queen and with her backing made Britain the most powerful nation on earth.

Felix Mendelssohn (1809-1847)

It is said of him that he "converted" out of expediency. However, evidence of his music and writings shows that he was a "completed" Jewish man. A world famous composer, pianist and conductor, he wrote such inspired pieces as the oratorios "Moses," "Elijah" and "St. Paul." As is true with most Jewish believers, he maintained a strong love for his people and did all he could to obtain their emancipation from the ghetto attitudes of the German people of that time.

Isaac Lichtenstein (19th century)

Lichtenstein was the District Rabbi of Tapio-Szele, Hungary. He became completed when he began idling through the pages of a New Testament which he had taken from a student some forty years previously. His completion caused a scandal in the Balkans and he was subject to persecution from many quarters. He never joined a church or accepted any support from a church, because he wanted the world to be certain that he did not accept Jesus as Messiah out of expediency. He expressed his desire in this way: "I would point the Jewish people to Jesus in His heavenly glory, in His divinity, exalted and great as eternity, as the Redeemer, the Messiah, the Prince of Peace."

When Lichtenstein first announced his belief that Jesus was the Messiah, the rabbinic leaders in Hungary offered to allow him to continue as a rabbi if he wouldn't preach the gospel in the synagogue. They offered to explain away his open profession of faith as "temporary insanity." He refused on the ground that what he had preached was the true Judaism, and that whereas he had been insane before not to see it, he had now come to his right mind.

Rabbi Max Wertheimer (19th century)

Born in Baden, Germany, Wertheimer was given intensive instruction in Orthodox Judaism, Hebrew and the Torah from an early age. After his Jewish schooling, he was put to work in the office of a manufacturer, but being on his own led him to drift away from his faith.

In order to save him, his parents decided to send him to school in America, where he attended Hebrew Union College in Cincinnati, Ohio. He studied the Old Covenant, Jewish History and the Talmud, eventually earning his master's degree. He was duly ordained a rabbi and officiated as such for ten years in Dayton, Ohio. He became popular as a public speaker, even in Christian churches. It wasn't until his wife died at an early age that he began seeking deeper answers to his questions about life and death. He began to study the Bible and especially the prophet Isaiah. Next he discovered that the Old Testament referred to God as *Yehoshua* or *Joshua*—in the Greek, *Yesous*. He was also forced to admit that in the Old Covenant the word *echod* always means a composite unity. Through the realization that this word is an integral part of the Jewish prayer *"Shmah Yisroel Adonai Elohenu Adonai Echod"* (Deuteronomy 6:4), the most important of all prayers, Wertheimer was finally brought to the conclusion that Jesus was the Messiah.

As a result of his confession of faith, he was dropped from the rolls of the Hebrew Union College and disowned by his people. He went back to school, became a pastor and served a Baptist church in Ohio. Although he was accused of becoming a Christian for monetary gain, he actually suffered severe financial losses by his move. Yet he counted it as nothing in the service of his Messiah.

Rabbi Aphraim ben Joseph Eliakim (1856-1930)

Born in the very heart of the Holy Land, in Tiberias by the Sea of Galilee, Rabbi Eliakim was early subjected to the teachings of the Torah and the Talmud. His father was a rabbi before him and as it was customary for the sons of rabbis to follow in their fathers' footsteps, it was natural that ben Joseph began his studies almost before he could walk.

Upon receiving his rabbinate he soon became a favorite of Arabs and Jews alike and, after he had married the daughter of the chief rabbi, settled down to live his life in honor and comfort.

He was fanatical in his hatred toward everything Christian, even refusing to permit his family to go to the mission hospital for medical care. If there were no Jewish doctors or facilities available, the family would receive no medical care, regardless of how ill they might be.

At that time, there was a loving Christian missionary in Tiberias who managed to befriend the rabbi and began showing him what true believers were really like. Eliakim slowly came to see the Bible with new eyes. Being deeply troubled, he went to his fellow rabbis for answers, but they began to be suspicious of him. When he finally became completed through a revelation from Jesus personally, he endured a time of fierce persecution.

Eliakim's faith was unfailing, however. Though his family was separated from him, he was baptized and moved to Jerusalem, where he went to work as a potter. His former students, who loved him deeply and who were now prominent rabbis in their own right, begged him to recant and return to the fold, but he refused.

Finally, the Lord rewarded Eliakim's faith and he became associated with the Christian Missionary Alliance as an evangelist to his people. He was given a meeting hall, and his Saturday night services were filled with unsaved Jews seeking the truth. Through the years repeated attempts were made to persuade him to renounce his Messiah, but all failed and he remained true to the Lord until his death.

So beloved was he that at his funeral Jews and Arabs together bowed their heads and thanked God for his ministry.

Albert Einstein (1879-1955)

It's open to question whether or not Einstein was a Christian. He repeatedly referred to himself as a Jew and at one time in his life reiterated it to a group of professors from Germany who asked him to "convert," so he could return to his native land and work in the universities there. Instead, he brought them a janitor, saying, "If it's a Christian you want, this is the best one I know."

Born in Ulm, Germany, he received his education in Switzerland and became a Swiss citizen in 1901. As a very young man he worked in a patent office in Berne and published four scientific papers, which made him internationally famous before he was 26 years of age. His paper on the Theory of Relativity revolutionized the world of science. In 1914, he moved to Berlin, but when Hitler came to power he emigrated to the United States and became a professor of theoretical physics at Princeton University.

Although Einstein never practiced the Jewish religion, he was always active in Jewish causes, especially that of Zionism. I have included him as a possible believer because of his professed attitude toward the Messiah. In an interview with reporters he said: "I am a Jew and nothing but a Jew. Of no one have I received instruction so much as from the Bible and the Talmud. I am a Jew, but I am dominated by the luminous figure of the Nazarene." He further stated that no one could "enclose Christianity in one word," and that he believed in the historicity of Jesus, "beyond any doubt." Throughout history God has manifested Himself to those who were this close to the truth. I myself am one of them, and I know many others. It pleases me to believe that this brilliant, kindly, gentle, decent man made it.

Simeon ben Zoma (first century C.E.)

Ben Zoma was one of the great Jewish sages, a contemporary of the Apostle Paul. According to Rabbi

Samson H. Levey, professor of rabbinics and Jewish religious thought at Hebrew Union College, ben Zoma may have become convinced through his studies of Christianity that Jesus was the Messiah. In those days, if a man had earned the right to be heard and to argue his opinion, his point of view was worthy of being preserved for posterity. Such opinions were recorded, no matter how unpopular they might be. Yet in ben Zoma's case his ideas were changed in the recording to make them appear different than they actually were. The claim was that he had lost his reason through extensive study of mystic lore. However, Rabbi Levey, through extensive study of other writings of the day, finds that ben Zoma taught about events and doctrines which are found in the New Testament. Among these were the virgin birth, the Trinity, the Last Supper, the crucifixion and resurrection and Jesus as God Incarnate (in human form).

Ben Zoma's apparent waywardness was concealed by contemporary sages and rabbis because of his brilliance and the influence he wielded over Jewish thinking of the day.

CHAPTER 6

Unusual Movements in the History of the Jewish People

Throughout the centuries my people have engaged in various movements which, in one way or another, have had great impact on the history of mankind. It is good for you to have some knowledge of these activities as an aid to your growth in *Yiddishe saichel* (Jewish-mindedness).

The Essenes

The Essenes were a sect of pious ascetic Jews whose lifestyle was similar to monks of today. They were not poor, as the property of anyone joining the group became the property of all. They earned a good living from the soil, preferred celibacy and did not permit women to join the group. They had great love for one another and rejected all pleasures as essentially evil. They did not go so far as to forbid marriage, but neither did they approve it. They believed that it was impossible for a woman to be faithful to one man and women kept men from being seriously devoted to the group. They frequently adopted children, however, if the children were young enough to be trained in the beliefs of the Essenes. They were contemptuous of wealth and, as all property belonged to the order, none of them was individually wealthy.

The Essenes were a democratic society, as is evidenced by the fact that those in charge of the wealth of the group were elected to office. They believed in the immortality of the soul, the resurrection of the body, and in the divine Messiah.

The Essenes date back before the Maccabees, to about 200 B.C. The order existed until approximately the end of the first century, A.D.

Possibly the most astounding thing about them was their belief in the "Teacher of Righteousness," who is supposed to have died around 60 B.C., having been put to death by the "Sons of Darkness." To them, he was the Messiah.

An Astonishing Similarity

The Dead Sea Scrolls reveal much about this Teacher of Righteousness, and his resemblance to our Savior is truly astounding. We like to think of *Yeshua* (Jesus) as being one of a kind. As the Son of God He truly was, but in the Teacher of Righteousness we see a forerunner of our true Messiah.

The Scrolls reveal that the Teacher of Righteousness preached penitence, humility, chastity and love of one's neighbor. He taught observance of the law of Moses and was opposed to the love of money or the acquisition of wealth in any form. He declared that the Law would be perfected by his own revelations and teachings. The Essenes considered him to be their redeemer and believed that he was the supreme judge of the dead. He was the object of hostility from the Sadducees and was eventually tried and put to death in Jerusalem. When he was near death, he called for the destruction of Jerusalem and, after it happened the Essenes believed it had come as punishment to the people for having killed him.

The followers of the Teacher of Righteousness practiced baptism and a form of communion. They were organized into groups similar to our churches. These had congregational organization, from which the government of Christian churches might have developed. Finally, the Teacher's followers were convinced he would return someday and bring an era of peace and joy.

Jesus, an Essene?

It is for the reasons discussed above that *Yeshua* (Jesus) has been declared by some to have been an Essene. But if one examines the matter closely and from a position of faith, rather than of intellect, the differences quickly become apparent. The history of Jesus' descent, the record of His virgin birth, His miracles, His claims to be Messiah, His fulfillment of Old Covenant prophecy, His claim that through Him we are saved, His prophetic descriptions of future events (almost all of which have now come true), His resurrection from the dead and ascension into Heaven, all clearly prove Him to be the Messiah, the Son of God.

Of course, the most important fact that proves Jesus

(*Yeshua*) to be the true Messiah is the experience of being "born again." It is also the most difficult to explain to unbelievers. Nevertheless, one should make every effort to explain the "born again" experience to unsaved people, both Jews and Gentiles, using verses such as Ezekiel 36:26-27 and II Corinthians 5:17, among others.

The Zealots

While the Essenes were practicing their out-of-this-world lifestyle, the Romans appointed a pack of fools to rule their Jewish subjects. They were guilty of the most heinous crimes against the people and against their moral and religious beliefs. They raised idols or statues of themselves or of Caesar in the temple. When the priests protested, they murdered them and their families. If rebellion was threatened because of these acts, they promised to recant, but as soon as the threat abated they murdered all those who had led the rebellion. They plundered the temple treasury and when the people protested they sent soldiers throughout the cities of Judea, who freely murdered the inhabitants, raped the women, sold the children into slavery, and generally plundered and pillaged everything in sight. The history of this time, when studied in detail, is absolutely appalling. Only the deeds of Hitler and his friends go beyond it. It should be remembered that Hitler attacked the Jews just because they were Jews. The Romans attacked the Jews because they were bestial fools who revelled in the opportunity to murder, rape, plunder and destroy.

As a response to this savagery a group called the Zealots emerged. They gradually gathered more and more Jews to their cause—to organize a rebellion against the Romans. As the atrocities continued, even some of the Jewish Christians of the day joined the Zealots. Finally, in A.D. 66 conditions became unbearable and the Jewish war with the Romans began. Lest I mislead you, I should like to make it clear that there were many thousands of Jews in Palestine who were strongly opposed to the rebellion, not only through fear of Roman power, but because Zealot behavior was not much better than that of the Romans.

Jerusalem, a Charnel House

For a time, the Jews were highly successful in their war against the Romans, but eventually Roman might caught up with them. The result was the total subjection of Judea and the destruction of Jerusalem and the temple. For really detailed information, one should read *The Jewish War*, by the historian Josephus.

Some idea of the extent of the slaughter can be seen in the record of the historian Tacitus that 600,000 innocent non-combatants were murdered just in the Roman mopping-up operation after the actual fighting was over.

You may think I am trying to point out the warlike tendencies of my people. Not so. What I want to emphasize is the opposite—that those ancient Judeans really would have been quite docile if the Romans had not been utterly brutal. Even under extreme Roman brutality most of the Jews under subjection were reluctant to fight and did their best to negotiate. The Romans utterly failed to appreciate and exploit the possibility of negotiation until after the battle was on.

With the war ending in victory for Rome, the activities of the Zealots virtually came to an end and little more is heard from them in the history of the Jews.

The Sadducees

According to the records the Sadducees were extremely rigid in their interpretation of the Law—and they elected themselves interpreters-in-chief. This gave them the opportunity to set up little rackets, such as, requiring the common people to use only Sadducee-approved animals in their temple sacrifices. Then they worked out a deal with those who sold these animals and birds (the money-changers) to kick back part of the proceeds to them. This was one reason for Jesus' anger at them (Matthew 21:12, 13). The people had to pay outrageous prices for these items in order for the Sadducees to get their cut.

Although the Sadducees had no belief in eternal life and did not accept oral law and tradition, they were powerful enough that most of the priests were elected from their numbers. Their followers included members of many of the wealthy families of Judea and also high level military leaders.

The Bad Guys

Politically the Sadducees were collaborators with their Roman rulers, and Annas and Caiaphas were even worse in this respect than the others (John 18).[1] This helps explain their blind stupidity.

---

[1] Nathan Ausubel, *Pictorial History of the Jewish People* (New York: Crown Publishers, 1953), p. 82.

What isn't generally understood is that the Sadducees were usually in conflict with the Pharisees. That's why they had to steal Jesus away in the middle of the night. If the Pharisees had known what was going on they never would have permitted such blatant violations of Jewish law and tradition.

The average Judean loved the Pharisees and hated the Sadducees. After the fall of Jerusalem and the destruction of the temple, when most of the rich and powerful had perished, the party of the Sadducees died out, never to reappear.

Before we leave the Sadducees, I would like to point out that since they didn't believe in eternal rewards and punishment, their natural philosophy was "Eat, drink and be merry for tomorrow we die, and after that, nothing." Jesus threatened to upset that applecart, so they sought His life. Through 2,000 years of their history, my people have paid a bitter price for the actions of the Sadducees—even though the Jews of their own era despised these people and were not unhappy to see them perish.

The Pharisees

In Matthew 5:17 and 18, Jesus tells us: "Think not that I have come to abolish the law and the prophets; I have not come to abolish them but to fulfill them. For truly, I say to you, till heaven and earth pass away, not an iota, not a dot, will pass from the law until all is accomplished." That is the same law most Pharisees studied, believed in and did their best to live by.

Paul, at the time of his completion, was not required to relinquish his rights and privileges as a Pharisee and

many years afterward he continued to lay claim to the
honor (Acts 23:6; Philippians 3:5).

And the Good Guys

Contrary to what Christian historians say about
them, the Pharisees, as a group, were not the prime
movers in the crucifixion of the Lord. At one time they
even tried to save Jesus' life (Luke 13:31). Although
they are mentioned as being involved in the later plot
against Him, most of the blame is placed on the Sadducees. We shall see why later. In the New Testament
we find that at least two of the Pharisees, Nicodemus
and Gamaliel, were quite helpful to new Christians
(John 7:50-52; Acts 5:33-39). History also teaches that
in the early days of the church the Pharisees often
endangered themselves on behalf of the Christians. For
instance, when James, the brother of the Lord, was
about to be executed the Pharisees attempted to in-
tercede on his behalf. And let us not forget that Paul
was a Pharisee (Philippians 3:5). What made the
Pharisees so much more reasonable than the Sadducees?
For this information we must go to the historian
Josephus and the *Babylonian Talmud*.

They Were So Close to Being Saved

Let me list some of the things the Talmud tells us
the Pharisees believed and taught. They knew:
> the principle of a plural Godhead (Mechilta to XV
> 26;46a and Joma 39a)
> that God is Spirit (Berakoth 10a)
> that man has a soul (Berakoth 10a)

that God operates outside of time (Megillah 14a)
and knows the future (Mechilta to XII 23;12a)

that God is compassionate but just (Aboth IV 29,
Genesis R. XII 15)

that men could not attain to the holiness of God by
their own efforts (Leviticux R. XXIV 9)

that there is a heaven and a hell (Ecclesiastes R. to
III 21)

that man is inherently sinful, but that it is possible
for one special man to be without sin and to be
immortal (Mechilta XVI 10;48a, Shabbat 55a)

that it is possible for men to have a personal
relationship with God and that God desires such
a relationship (Aboth III 18)

that repentance of sin brings divine mercy
(Deuteronomy R. II;12)

that man is saved by grace through faith (Makkoth
24a and Aboth III 19)

The Pharisees believed all these things, at least in-
tellectually, so you see how close they were to the Kingdom without being spiritually ready for it. The Sadducees, however, believed none of these things, so
naturally their credo was "Get it while the getting is
good." That made them greedy and lustful and
murderous, and this is why they were hated by the rank
and file.

Since the priests were members of the Sadducees
party, it is easy to see why *Yeshua* had so much trouble
with them and why the people flocked to His side.
Josephus tells us that the Pharisees far outnumbered the
Sadducees, and since they were held in high esteem by
the people they wielded a lot of power. Even the
Romans were careful in their dealings with them. The
Pharisees were a proud group and were very virtuous

and law-abiding. With the exception of the Apostle Paul before his conversion, we find in almost every biblical instance that the Pharisees were gentle in their dealings with the Lord and with Christians.

The Maverick

An emphasis on love and mercy was drilled into Paul as he grew up, but, for some reason, he went off in his private fanatical war against Christians. This was done with the connivance of the high priest (Acts 9:1), a Sadducee who had no scruples about what Paul was doing. It's unfortunate for Jews and Christians alike that so many historians have taken Paul's behavior to be the norm for the Pharisees. I can only point out that when Paul called himself "the chief of sinners" (I Timothy 1:15), he was judging himself by the standards of the Pharisees, as well as by his Christian faith. Before his completion (conversion) he had willfully broken every rule of human decency he and his people lived by and considered to be God's law. So, let's remember that Paul, when he was Saul, was a maverick. To equate all Pharisaic behavior with his is to malign a whole people, because the Jews of that time loved and followed the Pharisees. Such a belief also distorts Christian history, because it makes the Bible appear to convey ideas the writers didn't intend to convey.

It's true the Pharisees tried to test Jesus from time to time, but a study of their beliefs indicates they were being careful rather than malicious. They didn't want to mislead the people into following a false messiah. The danger that could accompany messianic delusions are clearly pointed out in the chapter on false messiahs. The

Pharisees were simply using their heads, although this is not apparent to Bible expositors who don't know their Talmud. The apostle Paul, when he was Saul, was an exception (the Talmud records other such exceptions).

Train Up a Child

Let's examine more of the basic principles Paul was taught as he grew up, keeping in mind that his training began when he was a mere toddler—the rabbis believed in the biblical command, "Train up a child in the way he should go, and when he is old he will not depart from it" (Proverbs 22:6). Paul was trained to believe that:

God knows our minds (Sanhedrin 90b)

God is compassionate and perfectly just (Berachoth 28b)

there is divine retribution for unrepentant sinners (Tosifta Joma V 9 and Aboth IV 29)

man should constantly be in an attitude of repentance (Shabbat 153a)

faith produces good works and the absence of good works is a sign of little faith (Taanith II I)

the righteous suffer for the sinful and *God himself* will atone for man's iniquities (Exodus R. XXXV 4)

brotherly love, charity, forgiveness, temperance, turning the other cheek, going the extra mile, suffering indignities without seeking revenge; returning good for evil—all these were required of man by God (Aboth III and Berachoth 17a).

These teachings also run through the Talmud:

human ways are the opposite of God's ways; it

is better to pray for the good of others than for one's own good; love, gentleness, kindness, meekness, submission, forbearance, remorse and penitence are demanded of us by God.

The Destruction of the Temple, A.D. 70

Most Jews and Christians know the temple was destroyed, but few know how this happened or what caused its destruction.

The events leading up to and culminating in the destruction of the temple and the razing of Jerusalem are a tale of man's perfidy and inhumanity. Volumes could be written about it, but I will try here to give you a general knowledge and understanding of the circumstances that brought on the disaster.

When the Romans first conquered Judea, they had sense enough to leave the Jews with a good deal of freedom, especially in religious matters. But, as time went on, this tolerance diminished, and real persecution began in the reign of Tiberius, 19 B.C. From that time on, taxes became unbearable, religious interference grew, and cruelty and injustice became the order of the day. The Roman policy was aided and abetted by puppet Gentile and Jewish rulers who sought only their own gain and cared little for the people. Jewish anger against the Romans slowly grew until it became uncontrollable. In A.D. 66 the rebellion broke out.

Those of us who have observed modern Israel are aware of the courage and determination with which Jews can fight when freedom is at stake. In A.D. 66 as in 1948, the rebels were weak in numbers, supplies and weapons. But what they lacked in these things they made up for in determination.

The War Is On

The first thing the Jews did was to take control of Jerusalem and begin to prepare for the seige which was sure to come. They also seized key points throughout the country and fortified them for a long war. Up to this point the Romans had been so confident of their power they had left these places under the control of small garrisons. Now, however, the Emperor Nero, became so alarmed that he sent his most able general, Vespasian (later emperor) to quell the rebellion.

God Takes Action for His Son's Sake

Let me digress for a moment to explain that if the Jews had succeeded in their revolt there would have been an upheaval throughout the empire, with rebellion breaking out everywhere. This is the reason for Nero's alarm. And it is also the reason for God's interference on the side of the Romans. If rebellion had succeeded throughout the empire the spread of Christianity would have been greatly slowed. The Romans had built roads, enhanced sea travel, organized the delivery of mail, and provided a measure of security for traveling throughout the known world. So, Paul and the other apostles, ministers, and teachers traveled in relative safety and had their letters delivered efficiently.

And the Romans Win

The campaign Vespasian mounted took four years and might not have succeeded had there not been treachery in the ranks of the Jews. Vespasian decided to conquer the fortresses one by one. The Jewish commanders thought this would exhaust his troops and supplies. They had a good plan, but it was undermined by Josephus, commander of the forces at Galilee and, later, official historian for the Roman Empire. After a pretense of putting up a good fight, he surrendered the province of Galilee to Vespasian. In his writings Josephus hotly denies this, but scholars generally disbelieve him in view of the fact that after the surrender of Galilee he joined the Roman forces against his own people. In A.D. 69, Nero died and Vespasian became emperor, leaving the command of the Roman forces to his son Titus.

Since the rest of Judea was now subdued, Titus advanced on Jerusalem. In the initial stages of the siege of Jerusalem Titus made every effort to allow the city to surrender with honor and dignity, but he was met with obstinate refusal. Even during the worst of the battle he repeatedly tried to obtain the surrender of the city through offers of mediation and mercy.

Meanwhile, the defenders of the city had split into three groups who, when not fighting Romans, were fighting each other. One group, under a man named Simon bar Giorah, were terrorists who looted, raped, and murdered anyone they thought disagreed with them. They insisted on fighting to the bitter end. Some citizens of Jerusalem were more afraid of them than they were of the Romans and wanted to surrender when Titus offered amnesty. They were murdered by Simon and his men.

The second group was led by John of Gischala. They were religious patriots, who wanted the freedom of the country for religious reasons and were willing to die for it. They were a larger group than Simon's, and they too were quite merciless in their dealings with the common people. The third group were the Sicarii, led by Eleazar bar Simon, who was simply a power-hungry opportunist.

Whenever the Romans broke off the attack to rest, replenish their supplies, or repair their war engines, these three factions turned on each other. The result was that when the Romans returned to the attack the Jews in the city were too exhausted to defend themselves with full strength. It also seems apparent that God intervened on the side of the Romans, as I mentioned earlier. For instance, Titus, who was a brilliant general, frequently exposed himself to the arrows and weapons of the Jews without his armor, and yet, he was never even wounded. The towers of Jerusalem were impregnable, as Titus himself stated later when he examined them, yet the Jews abandoned them for no apparent reason. The weather was unusually advantageous for the Roman side at that time of year. They were out in the open and there was a minimum of rain and cold to harass them.

Deuteronomy 28 Fulfilled

The descriptions that we have of the battle for Jerusalem are too horrible to need mentioning here. Suffice it to say that as a result of the onslaughts of the Romans and the fighting among the three factions, conditions within the city were deplorable. Because the population was starving, cannibalism occurred and disease was everywhere. Decaying bodies lay in the streets and the stench was almost overwhelming, even to the Romans outside the walls.

Nevertheless, the defenders fought valiantly. As the Romans breached the outside walls the people within built new ones, much to the chagrin of the attackers.

When the Romans finally gained a foothold within the city, old men and women and even young children fought to the death with great ferocity. As the end approached, one of the three factions within the city, the Sicarii under Eleazar, escaped and fled to a place called Masada, while the other two were walled up within the temple. Titus's forces finally broke through into the temple and the city was conquered. The carnage that ensued was one of the worst disasters ever to overtake any segment of humanity. The temple was destroyed by fire and the helpless citizenry brutally slaughtered. The remains of the temple were levelled to the ground. Those citizens who were left alive after the soldiers tired of the slaughter were sold into slavery or destroyed by wild beasts in the arena or in gladiatorial contests. John of Gischala surrendered, pleaded for mercy and spent the rest of his life in a Roman prison. Simon bar Giorah was executed.

The Beginning of the End for Rome

It took the Romans four years to put down the rebellion of the province of Judea. Historians record that when other captive nations saw the difficulties the Romans had with the Jews, they too began to think about rebellion. Thus began the slow but inevitable decline and fall of the Roman Empire, even though at the time it never seemed more secure.

Josephus reports that those who perished in the seige numbered over 1,100,000 souls. This means that the battle for Jerusalem was one of the costliest in history. There were four times as many deaths as those in the atomic bombings of Nagasaki and Hiroshima put together. Even after the downfall of the city, 11,000 more died of starvation and disease. The prisoners taken alive numbered 97,000, but no one knows how many of these survived.

After the fall of Jerusalem, a small band of Sicarii prepared to make a last stand against the Romans at Masada. Led by Eleazar, this group had been so indescribably evil toward their fellow Jews and even members of their own families that the people of Judea were happy to see them die. Rather than be captured, they committed suicide. They did this not so much out of bravery, but because they were afraid of what the Romans and their own people would do to them in revenge for their past deeds. Still, we must admit that to take their own lives rather than submit was an act of courage, especially when we have reason to believe that the Roman general, Silva, may have offered them clemency if they would submit, as was often the Roman practice of the day.

The Battle for Masada (ended May, A.D. 73)

Masada is nothing but a rock standing about 1500 feet high, with sheer walls and a flat top about three-quarters of a mile in circumference. The top is inaccessable, except for an extremely narrow path which, because of its twists and turns, is over three miles in length. The path has been slightly widened now, but in those days only the most agile climbers were capable of using it—the slightest slip meant death on the rocks below.

The edges of the flat top were lined by a wall 18 feet high and 12 feet wide. At intervals along the wall 37 towers were erected which were 75 feet high. These were connected by rooms and corridors within the wall. Josephus, the historian, reports that the surface was tillable and was used for farming. There were many large cisterns, and water was so abundant that they even had steam baths and a swimming pool. The climate was perfect for the preservation of food. In fact, when the Romans finally overcame the defenses of Masada they found food enough to last for many years. Even though this food had been stored for many years, it was still in perfect condition.

Defeat and Mass Suicide

The defenders of Masada numbered about a thousand, including women and children. From the Roman point of view the fortress had to be captured because it stood across valuable trade routes and because it would have encouraged rebellion in other parts of the empire if it successfully resisted the Roman forces. The attacking army was led by a Roman general named Silva. Silva found a cliff-life projection on one wall of the rock of Masada, 450 feet below the fortress. Using this as a work base, he built a ramp of earth from the base of the rock to the fortress. It took three years to construct this ramp, and much of it is still intact to this day.

All the time the ramp was under construction the battle went on, with the Jewish defenders hurling giant boulders or burning oil down on the Romans. The Jews had ample weaponry of all kinds, so the Romans were under constant attack and suffered heavy casualties. Nevertheless, they persevered and eventually breached the defenses of Masada. When the Jews within the fort saw that they were defeated, they committed mass suicide rather than submit to Roman brutality. The men killed the women and children and then killed each other. Only two women and five children escaped by hiding themselves in water conduits. These related what happened and so, the story of Masada became history.

The Marranos

After the fall of Jerusalem my people fled to many parts of the world. One of the most convenient places to find refuge was Spain. The climate was rather mild, it was fairly easy to get to from Judea, and while the Romans controlled Spain, they were too far away to be overbearing about it.

Spain is a country that has been passed back and forth between pagans, Moslems and Christians. I hate to tell you this, but for the most part, we Jews had it easy under the pagans and Moslems and tough under the Christians. Those early European believers seemed to have the notion that you could manufacture Christians with the use of machinery, such as the rack. What was manufactured was not Christians but Marranos— Jews and Gentiles who accepted Christianity for all the wrong reasons. Now, I must add here that I'm convinced that many of these Marranos were true believers. I Corinthians 12:3 tells us that no one confesses that Jesus is Lord save by the power of the Holy Spirit.

I believe that, and I believe it applied to many of the Marranos. Some of my people confessed the Messiah out of ambition or to escape the rack and got saved. But others became Christians only outwardly, while secretly practicing their Judaism.

Christian Love Brought True Completion

Forcible conversion was not constant throughout the hundreds of years of Jewish history in Spain. Many generations of Jews knew no persecution and during those periods my people prospered mightily. But inevitably, the old jealousies and hatreds seemed to crop up, and the good times would be replaced with bad.

In those early centuries large numbers of Jews did enter the church. In the sixth century over 95,000 of us became Christians. And in 1492, the year Columbus set sail for the East, 50,000 more did so, possibly to avoid expulsion by Ferdinand and Isabella.[2] There were 150,000 Jews in Spain at the time, and the 100,000 who refused to join the church became scattered all over the Mediterranean area. This act of expulsion certainly makes it appear that the 50,000 who stayed did so to avoid giving up their homes and careers. However, this was the height of the Inquisition, and Marranos, both Jewish and Moslem, were highly suspect. It is likely that many of these 50,000 new believers ended up being burned at the stake, rather than finding the new lives they sought.

As I travel about the country speaking and singing, I meet Christians who believe they are descended from

[2]Max I. Dimont, *Jews, God and History* (New York: Simon and Schuster, 1962), p.223.

those ancient Marranos and, therefore, have Jewish ancestry. That's why I believe many of those forced conversions were really completions. The Marranos asked Messiah to come in, for whatever reason, and He came in.

Ashkenazim

This name was applied to Jews of Germany and northern France beginning in the middle of the 10th century. After several hundred years it also came to be applied to Jewish people in other parts of eastern Europe.

It will help for you to understand how these Jews scattered over half of Europe came to be known as a movement called "Ashkenazic."

At the beginning of the 16th century, most European Jews had moved from western to eastern Europe, because life for them was easier there. Prior to this time, European society had been structured around the idea of serfdom. Serfs were considered to be the property of the nobles and were treated accordingly, having no rights worth mentioning. They were kept in ignorance and superstition lest they rebel against the lords and spoil the good thing those lovely gentlemen had going.

We Jews, however, were exempt from serfdom. We were too educated and had too many skills to be wasted in this way. The nobles, who were rather lazy, illiterate and ignorant themselves, needed us to run things. If serfs were taught to do skilled jobs, they'd quickly take over and that would be the end of the lords' advantages. We Jews, however, were outside of both classes, a sort of culture within a culture. We had the abilities that were in demand, so we were used by the nobles.

At first my people lived freely among the Gentiles, but gradually our laws and customs required that we move together into "Jewish areas." For instance, it was against Jewish law to ride on the sabbath, so Jews found it necessary to live close to the synagogue to make walking easier, especially for the aged and infirm. Since *yeshivas* (schools) were also located close to the synagogue, families tended to settle in Jewish clusters.

Schooled for Survival

My ancestors have always had sense enough to realize that survival depended on training. Their wisdom was borne out when the Reformation collided with Romanism. We Jews became pawns in this epic struggle. "Jewish areas" became ghettos where life was strictly regulated—unpleasantly by the nobles on the outside, and pleasantly by the rabbis on the inside. The Jews became more closely knit than ever, banding together under pressure, just as we do today.

If a Gentile landlord raised rents too high in a ghetto dwelling, the Jewish tenants moved in with friends or relatives and no one else would rent those quarters. Landlords soon got the message and the dwelling was re-rented to the original tenants at a more reasonable rate. This ability to win quiet battles caused Gentiles to view Jews with respect and Jews to view Gentiles with faintly contemptuous amusement.

The development of Jewish ghettos in Europe continued until the 19th century, when the struggle between the Catholic and Protestant churches began to simmer down and Jewish skills became more in demand because of the Industrial Revolution. It should be noted that ghettos were not prevalent in all of Europe—only in the North and East. When the Industrial Revolution gained momentum the people in these ghettos again spread across the continent, wherever their skills would bring them the best life. They and their descendants are known as "Ashkenazim" to this day.

Sephardim

These were primarily Spanish Jews who established a culture that spread throughout the Jewish communities of Spain, Portugal, France and Italy. This European Jewish culture lasted nearly a thousand years, beginning with the 7th century. It mixed the best of talmudic beliefs, traditions and customs, distilled them through half a dozen Mediterranean civilizations, refined them with Torah and set a pattern for Jews to live by until the 16th century.

When in 1492 we were expelled from Spain and scattered all over the Mediterranean world, Sephardic influences were weakened and the Ashkenazic movement became dominant. In brief, the Sephardim were dominant in Western Europe from A.D. 600 to 1500, when they were dispersed. From that time on Ashkenazic influences were stronger over the entire continent. Nevertheless, the Sephardim had a profound impact on my people, even to the point of influencing changes in the Hebrew language. Spanish Jews are still known as Sephardic and form a large part of the population of Israel.

Kabalah

Kabalah is a kind of Jewish mysticism. It was very influential during the Middle Ages, when my people felt the need of something to give them relief from the constant insecurity of being repressed and liberated, invited in and chased out, loved and hated.

Kabalists insisted that the Kabalah (their basic teaching) was given with the Torah, but in secret. Only a few special people were privy to its inmost secrets. Since it dealt in the occult, the common people who had little patience with Torah and Talmud flocked to it.

The Evil Eye

Kabalism emphasized numerology and divised ten rules, called divine radiations, by which men could establish God's existence in their lives. Its leaders also insisted the Messiah was coming any minute now and that His coming could be speeded up if Jews would follow Kabalah's rules of numerology, astrology, philosophy, Greek mythology, unscriptural prophecy, witchcraft, magic and spiritism. I rather hate to reveal Kabalism to you, since I'm trying to convince you we Jews are lovable. But this will help you see that we have really always been very human.

The Kabalists claimed they had a second oral law in addition to the Scripture. The movement was not respected by mainstream Jews until a book was published in the 8th century A.D. *The Book of Formation* concerned itself with so-called "godly experiences," which kept the understanding of Kabalism on a mystical plane. It wasn't until 500 years later that another book, *The Zohar,* brought Kabalism into a sort of theological focus by discussing God, science and the universe. For instance, it was believed that there was an "evil eye" that brought trouble on mankind. The books of the Kabalah explained how to ward off the "evil eye."

In spite of its Satan-inspired foolishness, the movement of Kabalism provided fertile ground for the beginning of real science in the Dark Ages. Its books were translated into various languages, including Latin, and many Gentiles who were familiar with its claims began thinking realistically along scientific lines. Great works in literature, science, art, philosophy, and mathematics can be traced to beginnings in Kabalism.

Superstition to Science to Salvation

The publication of *The Zohar* caused a split in the movement. The world was emerging from superstition to science. As this trend continued, the adherents of the mystic side of Kabalism became fewer in number, giving way to the realists and scientists. This branch of Kabalism continued to grow and flourish, coming more and more to the attention of the Gentile world. Finally, as Jewish and Gentile achievements slowly meshed, it became difficult to separate the two. So, Zoharist Kabalism eventually was swallowed up in the Scientific Revolution.

Meanwhile, mystic Kabalists became more secretive, which made it difficult for the common man to follow its rules. To keep him from deserting the ranks the mystics promised every century or so that Messiah's coming was at hand. Any movement which deals in hocus-pocus and broken promises hasn't long to live. By the 16th century the mystical branch of Kabalism had vanished from history. We don't have a count, but we know that many Kabalistic Jews became Christians. They had been promised a Messiah so many times, and been disappointed so many times, that they decided the "Gentile Messiah" might be the real one after all. *Ahlevai* (It should happen) again!

Hasidism

During the 18th century things deteriorated a great deal for Jews. Cossacks were murdering us for sport, peasants were killing us to relieve their own miseries, rulers were letting it all happen because for the time being they thought they didn't need us. Ignorance, power, debauchery, slavery and misery had again brought the world to a point where it needed a scapegoat. So they looked around and chose—guess who?

So Jews were again reduced to poverty and helplessness. That always seems to irritate God and He does something about it. (Isaiah 41:8-10).

This time He raised up a man, Israel ben Eliezer (1700-1760). Also known as Bal Shem Tov, "the Lord of the Good Name." He was an orphan and remained obscure until in his middle thirties he began to travel about the countryside performing miracles. This, together with his wisdom and piety, finally made him famous. He taught that it was more important to be joyous in the Lord and in the Torah than to be cold and unloving with knowledge of Law and Torah. In their unhappiness, my people accepted him enthusiastically and the Hasidic movement was born.

Ecstasy and Ignorance Take Over

Hasidism did its best to improve the lot of the common people. Instead of offering them mystical and occult experiences Hasidic teachers emphasized ecstasy. Unfortunately, in the process they also replaced the growing interest in science with a growing interest in ignorance. Hasidism assured the worst man on the block that he could reach a high state of contented spirituality by doing away with traditional Judaism and replacing it with Hasidic Judaism. It offered a personal relationship with God, but not according to God's way. If you said you had it, you had it. That's all there was to it.

Deprivation and distress were no longer seen as deprivation and distress, so the deprived and distressed among my people readily embraced Hasidism. At one time, half the Jews of Europe were Hasidic, and that means Bal Shem Tov had over a million followers. But the movement lacked sound leadership and guidance. And its followers found that after the initial period of joy through ecstasy the same old miseries cropped up. Their disillusionment with Hasidism proved once again that the only way to come to God is God's way, through Messiah.

Too Many Generals

When Bal Shem Tov died in 1760, there remained about 150,000 Hasidim, but from then on the movement rapidly declined. A number of new leaders asserted themselves, each moving in his own direction and doing his own thing, because there were no rules. A leader would gain power for a time and enjoy tem-

porary success. This attracted other potential leaders
and the process was repeated over and over again until
all unity was destroyed and the Hasidic movement
collapsed.

Today, the movement has only a few adherents, but
these modern Hasidim have wholeheartedly returned to
Torah and Talmud and are among the most orthodox of
all Jews.

Background for the Founding of Modern Israel

As the centuries rolled by, Jewish life followed a
predictable pattern. Jews were invited to immigrate to
various countries, because their skills were needed.
When those skills were no longer needed they were
ordered to leave. Rulers arose who had compassion on
them, followed by others who butchered them. These
things occurred in every nation in Europe and under
every sort of political or religious rule. Sometimes, we
were simply caught in the general mayhem.

For instance, the Inquisition was not primarily
aimed at Jews, but at all those who were considered to
be heretics by the church in Spain. Many Spanish Jews
(called "Marranos") had joined the church, but they
were still suspected of secretly following their former
religion. As the Inquisitors were not too particular about
really determining guilt, many of the Marranos who had
truly joined the church perished, along with millions of
Protestants. For a long time the Inquisition took no
action against Spanish Jews who had not joined the
church. Later, however, these Jews also became victims,
because many of them were related to Marranos, or
were thought to be an unwholesome influence on them.

As has so often been the case in history, persecutors soon lose control of themselves and helpless people become victims for no other reason than that they are helpless. Despite these calamities, the Jewish people remained a cohesive group, moving from country to country as they could, asking nothing but to be allowed to live and let live.

The Birth of Modern Israel

Through all these centuries of the Dispersion the thought remained in the minds of my people that one day they would return and dwell in Israel, even as the Old Covenant predicted (see Deuteronomy 30:3-5, Jeremiah 32:37, many others). This belief was turned into action at the time of the Dreyfus case (see chapter 5).

Around the beginning of this century, meetings began among world Jewish leaders whose aim was to establish a Jewish national homeland in Palestine. Great impetus was given the movement in 1917, when the British Foreign Secretary, Arthur J. Balfour, declared his sympathy for Zionism. By 1922, the United States Congress had issued a declaration in favor of the establishment of a Jewish national homeland in Palestine, and President Harding signed it. Finally, in 1924 the League of Nations voted to give Britain a mandate to carry out the Balfour Declaration.

Britain no sooner had the mandate than she began to back away from her commitment. In 1937 she proclaimed publicly that the Balfour Declaration had been made to win the support of world Jewry in the war with Germany and that during 1915 the British government had entered into an agreement with the Arabs. This guaranteed Palestine to them in exchange for an Arab attack on Turkey, which was about to enter the war on the German side.

During World War I, the Jewish population of Palestine had been reduced by fifty percent as a result of natural causes, war, famine, and Arab attacks. However, after the Armistice was signed, the Jewish population began to increase again, and this aroused the Arabs even more. By 1930 a state of anarchy existed. This so alarmed the British they barred further Jewish immigration to Israel, despite the Balfour Declaration and the League of Nations mandate.

And the Struggle for Liberation

While these events were going on, the Jews in Palestine, realizing they had no other protection, banded together and formed a defense group. This organization was known as the Haganah, and by 1936 it numbered at least 25,000 men and women. In addition to the Haganah there were two major terrorist groups known as the Irgun and the Stern Gang. These, however, lacked general support because of their violent activities.

In 1939, the British issued a white paper attempting to force a compromise between the warring factions. All this did was enrage the Arabs and disenchant the Jews. In it immigration to Palestine was severely limited. The Arabs wanted no Jewish immigration at all and the Jews wanted complete freedom of immigration, so the compromise pleased no one. Jewish anger resulted in increased support for the terrorist gangs, who now declared war on the British, the Arabs, and anyone else who threatened Jewish immigration to Palestine.

Hitler's "Solution to the Jewish Problem"

Then came what we Jews now call "The Holocaust." World War II had broken out in Europe, and the Nazis had embarked on what they called, "the final solution to the Jewish problem." Why Jew-haters always think their hatred of us is our fault has always been a mystery to us Jews. From the time Hitler came to power until the end of the war this was the assumption of the German leaders. Elaborate gas chambers were built so Jews could be exterminated more rapidly and efficiently. Masses of Jews were forced to dig their own graves and were then shot in such a way that their bodies fell into the holes they had just dug. Men were forced to shoot their wives and children under the threat that if they didn't their families would be tortured until they died. Women and young girls were forced into houses of prostitution for the Nazi army until they contracted venereal disease; then they were unceremoniously put to death. Brutal experiments were conducted to determine the amount of pain the human body could endure before it succumbed, or to see if it could function without muscles. One charming Nazi lady, Ilsa Koch by name, made lampshades out of the skins of her victims.

In the end six million Jews perished—forty percent of the entire Jewish population of the world. Anyone with more than 10% Jewish blood was eligible for execution, Jewish Christians included. And let us not forget that thousands of Christians died with them, plus gypsies and anyone else the Nazis deemed unworthy to live in their "*Reich* that would last a thousand years," as Hitler put it.

Yeshua Saves!

Those of us who lived in other parts of the world were more fortunate. The Lord gave strength and determination to real Christians so they were able to fight and destroy this evil, so that our lives and culture were preserved. They did it because they loved us for the sake of Messiah and because of the blessings our unusual gifts have meant to them throughout the ages.

After World War II, as a result of the Nazi Holocaust, there was a tremendous wave of immigration of Jews to Palestine. This quickly aggravated the situation. Violence grew, with the British trying to control it and usually favoring the Arabs. Finally, in July, 1946, the Irgun bombed the hotel in which the British had their government offices. Many were killed and the British commander, in exasperation, ordered the English troops to boycott Jewish shops. He declared that this would hit the Jews in their pocketbooks where it would hurt most, "thus showing our contempt for them." While this declaration resulted in an international furor, the bombing itself turned the Palestine Jews against the Irgun and efforts to curb it began. However, the overall struggle to establish a Jewish national homeland in Israel continued unabated.

Murder and Violence Again Run Rampant

Now the country was paralyzed. Violence was rampant and the British were unable to control it.

In 1947, after the English announced they were no longer able to cope with the situation, the United Nations settled on a plan to partition Palestine between Jews and Arabs. The Jews agreed with reservations, but the Arabs rejected the plan outright and reacted violently. In two weeks they killed 2,000 Jews—men, women and children.

The United Nations had sent a commission to supervise the partition of the country, but they too were helpless before the violence. Four times they complained to the United Nations that the British were refusing to cooperate and that if something wasn't done war would break out. Nothing happened. At last, the Haganah realized it would have to fight and began to mobilize and prepare for war.

The story of the war for liberation fills many books and needn't be retold here. The Arabs, with their vast population, thought they could quickly defeat the Jews. They were mistaken. As a Christian, I see in this the Lord God almighty fighting on behalf of Israel, just as He promised. Some Christians disagree. They feel I take the attitude I do because I'm Jewish, but I believe the majority of Gentile Christians believe likewise.

At Last! A Homeland

After many months of violent fighting, the Jews finally established their control over the country and in May of 1948, the United Nations finally recognized the nation of Israel.

Most of the Arab population of Israel fled at the instigation of their leaders, but the Arab nations surrounding Israel attacked with all the strength at their command. The Haganah, solidly backed by the people, fought them off and finally in 1949, realizing it was hopeless to fight on any longer, the Arabs signed an armistice with the new nation.

That armistice has been broken many times in a number of minor battles and in three major wars. In 1956, when Israel, France and England invaded Egypt over the Suez Canal, that invasion was quickly stopped and the troops withdrawn because of the violent opposition of the United States under the Eisenhower regime. The armistice was broken again in 1967, in what is now known as the Six-Day War, and in 1973 during Yom Kippur. These wars will be discussed later on.

The Battle of the Warsaw Ghetto

The story of the Warsaw Ghetto is typical of what happened in many ghettos throughout the German occupied territories during World War II. Germany had no sooner invaded Poland in September of 1939, than she began a roundup of Warsaw Jews and herded them into an area 100 square blocks in size. By November, an announcement was made that the operation was complete. Almost half a million Jews were now confined in this area, and the process of exterminating them began. They were all subject to slow starvation, but for some the slow death process was speeded up by removal to the gas chambers.

Many have asked me why they didn't resist from the very beginning. The answer is simple. They couldn't believe what was happening. Neither did the rest of the world at first.

Truth Will Out

When reports filtered into the ghetto about the wholesale slaughter in gas chambers, the people living there doubted their truth. But as such reports continued to come in from Jewish and Gentile underground fighters the people finally realized that they were true. From that time on, the Jews decided to die fighting and resistance was organized. By this time only 40,000 Jews remained in the ghetto, and these were all sick and weakened from prolonged deprivation and starvation. However, they held off the German armed forced for 42 days. Fighting with such weapons as they had managed to beg, borrow or steal from sources such as the Polish underground and Polish sympathizers, they made it necessary for the Germans to bring in a Panzer division, heavy artillery, and the air force.

The Battle for the Warsaw Ghetto began in April of 1943, and the Germans declared it over on May 16th. Actually, sporadic fighting went on for several weeks more, with Jewish suicide squads fighting from the rubble. In some cases they had nothing but clubs and stones.

In the end, the artillery and bombs killed all but several hundred Jews who escaped to underground units by crawling through sewers, neck-deep in slime. They left behind them over 5,000 dead Germans. Not one of the Jews surrendered. All either died fighting or escaped.

Of Mice and Men

Unfortunately, there were among the Jews of Warsaw a few who attempted to save themselves by collaborating with the Germans. In the end they too went to the gas chambers or, stricken by conscience, committed suicide.

There is a general belief that my people went meekly to their deaths in the concentration camps. The record shows otherwise. Here are a few examples. The Jews in the Vilna ghetto fought off the German forces for a week before finally being annihilated. Jewish guerrilla bands harassed the German forces continually in central Europe. At Treblinka concentration camp the inmates rebelled in August, 1943, overpowered and killed all the camp personnel and escaped into the forest, after destroying the camp by fire. Most were recaptured, but some were able to join guerrilla bands and fought the Germans to the end of the war.

There are recorded instances of Jewish women arming themselves with homemade hand grenades and at the moment of entering the chambers throwing themselves on their German guards, killing the guards and themselves.

No one will ever know how many allied lives were saved by such actions nor how much the war was shortened by the bravery of these people.

The Six-Day War

This war is so recent most people remember the events leading up to it. But it will not take long for those events to fade into memory, so I would like to recount them briefly.

From the time Israel was established in 1948, tensions between Jews and Arabs mounted steadily. The Arabs claimed Israel belonged to them by reason of hundreds of years of occupation. The Jews made the same claim and for the same reason, saying that they had been established there before the Arabs by the Almighty Himself. Most real Christians today back the claims of the Jews. Most, but not all.

The anger and frustration of the Arabs continued to mount until finally, in June of 1967, aided and abetted by Russia, the Arabs attacked Israel from all sides. They were defeated and driven back in six days. I see no point in giving a complete history of that war, but it is interesting, especially to Christians, to recite some of the more unusual aspects of it which indicate the hand of God at work in the life of the nation of Israel.

ITEM: Many jokes have been circulated about Arabs dropping their weapons, deserting their tanks and trucks, and fleeing the scene of battle, leaving much of their Russian equipment intact. They were terrrified, but why should this be? Arabs are as good fighters as anyone else and have proved it many times throughout history. At one time, they conquered all of North Africa and a large part of Europe. So why this fearfulness?— unless God interfered on the side of His chosen people as He has so often in the past.

ITEM: In the Golan Heights, which were held by Syria, the Israelis had to fight their way up steep hills to dislodge the Arabs, yet they were able to do so very quickly. The Arabs were better armed and equipped and had fortified the hills with trenches and pillboxes. They had also chained their soldiers to their artillery so they couldn't run away. However, there was no cohesion in command, Arab communications broke down, orders that did go through were conflicting, utter confusion reigned in Arab ranks. The result was that Israel conquered the Golan Heights in record time and with a minimum of casualties.

ITEM: The Israeli Air Force utterly destroyed the Egyptian Air Force while it was on the ground. In one sector the Israelis lured the Egyptians into the air, so as to cause them to warm up their planes. It seems the Israelis were using heat-seeking missiles and if the Arab planes were not warmed up the missiles wouldn't work. When the Arab planes were airborne the Israelis turned back to Israel. The Egyptians returned to Egypt, parked their warmed-up airplanes, and went off to breakfast. But then the Israeli pilots returned and released their missiles which promptly zeroed in on and destroyed those parked Arab planes.

ITEM: In one section of an important valley the Arabs became so interested in a German television crew that was there to record the important battle that they quit fighting. Hundreds of them were captured without a shot being fired.

ITEM: In the Gaza Strip Arab men stood by the roadside with their arms in the air and their eyes shut tight, waiting to be shot. They actually believed what they had been told—that the Jews would murder them all if they won. Imagine their surprise and delight when they were sent to college instead.

ITEM: At one point in the war, over 400 Arabs were captured by only two or three Israeli soldiers. After they had surrendered and laid down their arms, they seemed surprised that there were so few Israelis. "Where are the others?" they kept asking. When questioned further, they claimed they had seen thousands of Israeli soldiers "all dressed in white." This should be no surprising thing to any real born again Christian, but it certainly was surprising and confusing to the Israelis.

So, these are some of the stories that have come out

of the Six-Day War. They seem to indicate that God was in charge all the time. We believers can say "Amen" to that.

The Yom Kippur War

On October 6, 1973, *Yom Kippur* (the Day of Atonement), a day which in Israel is especially sacred so that all activities are at a standstill, the Egyptians and Syrians attacked Israel on their respective fronts. While not taken by surprise, the Israelis were at a disadvantage because of their holiday. Even so, after two weeks of fighting, the Israelis were again winning. At that point the United States and Russia intervened and, with the aid of the United Nations, effected a ceasefire. At this writing, negotiating is still going on, with threats to renew the fighting coming from the Arab side continuing.

In this war the Arabs had the finest equipment the Russians could provide and the advantage of attacking on a day when my people are at worship and not prepared to do any fighting. (The ancient Romans were also adept at taking advantage of Jewish holidays to win battles.) In spite of their advantages, the record shows that the Arabs did things which are directly contrary to good sense and established rules of warfare.

How Not to Fight a War

The Los Angeles *Times* for November 5, 1973, reports: "Israeli generals waited to see how the major Egyptian attack would shape up. Incredibly, it never did." In other words, they failed to press their advantage after the first surprise attack. The paper further reports, "The Egyptians failed to employ a cardinal tactic of warfare: concentration of forces. . . . The Egyptians' tanks outdistanced their mechanized infantry, thus losing the support of the handheld anti-tank missiles that had previously been so successful." The military analysts say that the Israeli crossing of the Suez Canal was evidently treated as a propaganda stunt and wasn't taken seriously until the Egyptian third army was completely encircled and cut off.

By the time the cease-fire was forced on Israel, its army had moved to the west bank of the canal in force and was in a good position to conquer all of it.

From the same Los Angeles *Times*: "The Israeli high command admits that the Arabs improved noticeably, but the end result indicates that the Israelis still maintain their qualitative advantage."

The final outcome of all this is still in the future, but there is enough evidence to indicate that something still happens to the Arabs when they undertake to destroy Israel. They just don't seem to be able to keep their military heads on straight. Real Christians will agree with me the answer is—God.

The Long Distance Runner

At this juncture in time, United States Secretary of State Vance is running madly to and fro among the nations in an effort to obtain a lasting peace. And Soviet Russia seems to be anxious for peace, too. Their need for American food and knowhow dictates their behavior.

To those who know Biblical prophecy it seems likely this will change in the near future. While all normal people yearn for peace, we Christians know there will be no peace until the Messiah comes. The entire Middle East situation proves it.

A quick look at a map tells how easily the problems in this area could be solved, if only there wasn't so much hatred involved. The climate is excellent and improving; the ground is fertile and growing more so. The entire area could be a garden again if the fighting would stop and the hard work begin. Israelis have proved this by turning the areas they control into a model of productivity. And Israel has stated she would help the Arab countries improve their living standards if they would let her live in peace. I believe them, but then, I'm Jewish. I know my people and I think I am very objective about them—and I believe them.

CHAPTER 7

Questions and Answers

Most non-Jews try to compare the Jewish people with other branches of humanity. This is not possible. History has proven us to be a unique entity unlike any other group on the face of the earth. If we weren't we'd be extinct like the Hittites. Unremitting efforts to destroy us through assimilation, conversion (forcible conversion does not always result in "completion") or just plain murder testify to Satan's unrelenting hatred for us. But here we are, and *that* testifies to God's unrelenting determination to preserve us, not only for the sake of our forefathers (Romans 11:28) but also in order that our descendants may spread the gospel in the Great Tribulation (Revelation 7).

It is because of this distinctiveness that I have included a chapter in this book devoted to the answering of questions which have not been dealt with earlier. My purpose is to enable you to to show my people how much you love them.

Obviously, it isn't possible to answer all the questions one has about the Jewish people, but I will touch on the ones I've heard over and over again. If they are helpful, let me know. That will encourage us to publish some more answers to questions later on.

How can one tell if a person is Jewish?

There is no way! Many claim they can always tell, but what really happens is that when they meet a Jewish person who doesn't fit their conception of what a Jew is, they just don't recognize him to be Jewish. Or, put another way, if we don't fit the stereotype the world has about us, they think we're Gentiles.

The truth is that there are spiritual forces at work here most people don't recognize. When Christians love the Jewish people, God sees to it that the Jewishness of people they encounter is revealed to them in due time. On the other hand, when a person hates Jews, Satan sees to it that Jewish individuals become apparent to them as quickly as possible.

If you're a Christian who behaves as a Christian should, you'll be surprised at how my people will let you know who they are.

Is the Jewish Bible different from the Christian Bible?

Yes, in that it doesn't contain the New Testament portion. Also, the books are arranged differently and some of the verses vary in their numbering. There are also some slight differences in references to the Messiah. *It is best to use the official Jewish version* if one wishes to witness from the Jewish Bible, because most other Jewish translations are really paraphrased versions and contain serious distortions. The title of the official Bible is: *The Holy Scriptures, in English, according to the Masoretic Text,* published by the Jewish Publication Society of America.

What is the Jewish opinion of the writings of the prophets?

Their opinions are as diversified as they can be and range from total acceptance (the Hasidim) to total non-acceptance (Reform Judaism). *Very generally speaking,* most modern Jewish people will have very little understanding or knowledge of the prophets, but will respect *the idea* of the prophets as a part of Jewish tradition.

Are religious Jews easier to reach than non-religious?

That is entirely a matter of personality and the prejudices stemming from bitter experiences. Many Orthodox rabbis have found *Yeshua* to be the Messiah through their expert knowledge of Torah and Talmud. And they did so in ages when Jewish persecution was at its zenith. "The word of God is living and active . . . piercing to the division of soul and spirit, of joints and marrow" (Hebrews 4:12, RSV). *Yeshua* is the Word (John 1:1) and He also is Love (I John 1:8), so it follows that the Christian who loves and uses the Word is going to reach the innermost being of those to whom he witnesses. That's the key.

What is meant by good or bad witnessing?

Any witness that isn't led of God and administered out of love will lead to the pitfalls of the flesh that Satan

expertly puts in our path. On the other hand, a witness
that is led of God and filled with love is going to be
blessed, even though it may not appear to be effective
at the time. The Bible reassures us: "The Spirit inter-
cedes for the saints according to the will of God"
(Romans 8:27b, RSV). And the Talmud adds: "Whoever
helps Israel is as though he helped the Holy One . . ."
(Mechilta to XV. 7; 39b); "Whoever hates Israel is like
one who hates Him" (Sifre Numbers 84; 22b).

What is pre-Bible witnessing?

When real Christians make an effort to gain the love
and trust of their Jewish friends this might be called
pre-Bible witnessing. Such an effort is usually helpful,
because so many Jewish people are not emotionally
ready to listen to the gospel when first approached.
Their past experiences with so-called Christians are too
studded with bitter and painful memories to allow for
open-mindedness. The effect of these past experiences
must be overcome with a steady display of Christian
love and respect before Jewish people who have had
these experiences can be expected to listen. But be of
good cheer. The Talmud says: "Thou shalt love thy
neighbour as thyself. I [God] created him; and if you
love him, I am faithful to repay you a good reward; but
if you do not love him, I am the Judge to exact a
penalty" (ARN XVI). And the Messiah said: "I have
said this to you, that in me you may have peace. In the
world you have tribulation; but be of good cheer, I have
overcome the world" (John 16:33, RSV). So, there are
great rewards in store for those who love, and those rewards are even more beautiful for those who *overcome*

themselves (their own prejudices) to do it. And remember, the instant you take a step in the direction of loving people into the Kingdom, God is there to help.

What should be kept in mind when entertaining mixed groups to which Jewish people have been invited?

Above all, the Christian should invite only those Gentiles who are completely free of any anti-Jewish sentiment. Careful arrangements should be made that any activities in the course of the evening will not hurt Jewish sensitivities, even indirectly. No stories should be told involving Jews or with Jewish accents. No games should be played that obliquely refer to Jewish customs or habits. If food is served and a blessing is asked, the blessing should be asked in the name of the Messiah, or in the name of the Lord, or even *Yeshua*, but do not ask it in the name of Jesus or Christ.

Do Jewish people have a good foundation in the Torah and Talmud?

This is one of the great fallacies Satan has fostered in order to make real Christians self-conscious in their outreach to my people. After all, if you're not well-grounded in Scripture *and think you're talking to someone who is,* you're bound to be a bit uneasy about what you're claiming. Just remember, unsaved Jews are unsaved people, and unsaved people usually have very little interest in Scripture. I should point out, however, that one may meet people, both Jews and Gentiles, who are very well-versed in Torah and Talmud even though they are unsaved.

Are Jews set apart because of their background and heritage?

This may have been true in earlier days, especially in Europe. In those times, there were vast cultural and ideological differences between Jews and Gentiles. In the Western world today those differences do not exist, as Jewish people generally are well-assimilated into the Western way of life. However, they are not readily accepted on a more intimate basis among unsaved Gentiles. In Christian society their assimilation has been increasing in recent years because Christians have been active in showing love, understanding and patience in their relationships with Jewish people. They have also been going out of their way to learn about the culture and background of their Jewish loved ones. If this is not true, why are you reading this book?

Despite the fable that we Jews are clannish and deliberately avoid associating with outsiders, it is not traditional for us to behave in this way. While the Talmud teaches that we must learn to be self-reliant, it also teaches that we owe something to all mankind, because God created us all. Hence, it is written, "Separate not yourself from the community" (Aboth II.5), and, "A man's mind should always be harmoniously attuned to that of his fellow creatures" (Kethuboth 17a).

This assumes that the non-Jewish person is doing likewise. It's impossible to attune your mind with that of someone who hates you simply because you're Jewish, or black, or Catholic, or whatever. All through our history we Jews have become absorbed into the general community whenever we have been allowed to do so. This is happening right now in the United States.

Statistics show there are a quarter of a million less Jews now than there were right after World War II. What are the causes? Intermarriage and just plain lack of interest in things Jewish.

Do the Jewish people believe the Messiah is yet to come?

Generally speaking, Orthodox and Conservative Jews still believe that the Messiah will yet make a first appearance. Reform Jews, however, are rejecting this idea, in many instances even claiming that Bible references to a coming Messiah do not actually refer to a person but to a messianic age in which there will be universal peace and brotherly love.

Do some Jewish people deny they're Jews?

Yes, but just a few. Some become Christians and assimilate into the church completely, and that's the last that is heard of them. At this time, however, others of us feel it is crucially important for the Jewish Christian to maintain his Jewishness within the church. This helps his unsaved fellow Jews understand they will not be alone if they accept the Messiah.

There's an old Jewish proverb: "*A meshumed iz nit keyn Yid un nit keyn goy*" (A convert is no Jew and no Gentile). If we are ever to reach large numbers of the truly Jewish Jews for their Messiah, we must first prove that this saying has no validity, especially since in the past it did indeed have so very much validity.

Since many Gentiles do not attend church, doesn't this indicate to the Jewish people that there is a difference between Gentiles and Christians?

No. Many Jewish people do not attend the synagogue. Nevertheless, they are still considered Jews. The Jewish person can be a true Jew without practicing the Jewish faith. Therefore, the Jewish people assume that a Gentile can be a Christian without practicing the Christian faith. To the Jewish people all Gentiles are Christians, just as all Jews are Jews, including communists, atheists and the like. It seldom occurs to my people that there is a contradiction in calling an atheist, Communist or Nazi a Christian. This sort of thinking is prevalent in the non-Christian world generally. Many people think that all one must do to be a Christian is be born a Gentile.

Is it wrong for a Gentile to imitate the popular conception of a Jewish accent?

In my opinion anyone who has an accent is liable to be sensitive about it. Furthermore, down through the ages notorious Jew-haters have used the concept of a Jewish accent to prove that Jewish people are strange and different. And those who cling to Satan's world are always eager to react strongly against those who aren't "like us." Since this accent nonsense has always been used as a weapon against us Jews, the latent fear we have of Jew-haters may possibly be fully aroused when we hear a Gentile speaking in this manner. I call it "accent nonsense," because it is ridiculous for anyone to hate another person because of his speech patterns.

There are few Jewish people who have escaped being accused of having this so-called Jewish accent, even though the majority of us do not. But there are Gentiles who have it—and how! The accent results from a combination of circumstances, especially from the effort to speak English against a background of eastern European languages. In extreme cases it has a sing-song quality similar to that which is inherent in Jewish prayer ritual. It also may have an unpleasant sound to Gentile ears, because the language characteristics of Yiddish and Hebrew have a tendency to give a harsh sound to languages such as English which are so completely unlike them. Gentile Christians who love the Jewish people would do well to leave the imitation of Jewish accents to professional comedians. They are mostly Jewish, and that makes the use of accents a family joke.

Is there a difference between Jews and Hebrews?

The origin of the word "Hebrew" is in doubt. In the Bible the first person to be called a Hebrew is Abram (Abraham—Genesis 14:13). But the word may only mean that Abram "crossed over" the Euphrates and not that God was hanging a label on him. "Hebrew" may be derived from "Eber" (Genesis 10:21, 22), the name of one of Abraham's ancestors. Or it may come from the Hittite word *Habiru* meaning "to cross over."

In any case, after Abraham crossed the Euphrates, he and his descendants through Isaac and Jacob were known as Hebrews (Genesis 40:15; 43:32). Many scholars today insist that modern Jews are descendants of Judah and Benjamin and, therefore, it isn't correct to call them Hebrews, but "Jews" (from Judah). However, since those tribes are descended from Abraham, Isaac and Jacob, it would seem legitimate to speak of them as "Hebrews" also.

Frankly, there's little point in debating which is technically correct. What is important is that many of us have been called names which were crudely attached to the word "Hebrew," so we are touchy about it. Although many Jewish Christians call themselves "Hebrew Christians," we suggest you stay away from the word. For reasons already explained, it is better to use the term "Jewish people," than "Hebrew people," or "Hebrews." Why make waves?

Are Jewish people still looking for fulfillment through faith?

Not the majority of them. It's too difficult for them to learn the truth through their religious practices. They leave them unsatisfied. If Christians will approach them with patience, love, and understanding, Jewish people will listen to what they have to say. As it is written, "Provide yourself with a teacher [of Torah] and you will get yourself a companion, and judge all men in the scale of merit" (Talmud, Pirke Aboth 1.6.).

Are Jewish people generally liberal when it comes to national policies?

It is traditional for my people to feel that emotional security is best obtained by making healthy contributions to society. So we try to do the best we can in whatever we choose as a vocation. Besides, the Talmud, and therefore our Jewish heritage, demands that we must do all we can to help our fellow man, whoever he may be, and regardless of his feelings toward us or ours toward him. Hence, there are extensive worldwide Jewish social activities of all kinds, and they are available to all in need.

This also makes a majority of us lean toward that political party which we feel is most sensitive to the needs of the ordinary person. Conservative politicians, it is felt, are not so concerned about the immediate needs of the middle and lower classes. We should all remember that *this belief is common among the majority of Americans today,* especially those who belong to minority groups. The Talmud proclaims that a person isn't privileged to drill a hole in the bottom of a boat just because the hole is only under his own seat (Leviticus Rabbah IV 6). In other words, in time of trouble each of us is responsible for all others. That tradition seems to govern most Jewish Americans' approach to politics.

A Closing Word

In my many visits to churches I have seen that most of those which have had no outreach to my people have also had little power and growth. On the other hand, those who have cared, really cared, about them have experienced vital, growing ministries. This is because God has decreed that it shall be so. In reading this book and acting on its advice you are responding to His will as it was ordained for you to do almost three thousand years ago:

"The Lord will have compassion on Jacob and will again choose Israel, and will set them in their own land, and aliens will be joined with them and will cleave to the house of Jacob" (Isaiah 14:1).

Christians today have a job to do in the Lord and, thank God, they've begun to do it. James tell us, "Faith by itself, if it has no works, is dead" (2:17, RSV). And the Talmud adds, "This world is like a vestibule before the World to Come; prepare yourself in the vestibule that you may enter into the hall" (Aboth VI 21).

God bless you as you get on with it.

Shalom